VEGAN
Baking

VEGAN
Baking

MORE THAN 50 RECIPES FOR VEGAN-FRIENDLY
CAKES, COOKIES & OTHER BAKED TREATS

DUNJA GULIN

photography by
Clare Winfield

RYLAND PETERS & SMALL
LONDON • NEW YORK

Senior Designer Toni Kay
Commissioning Editor
  Céline Hughes
Head of Production Patricia
  Harrington
Editorial Director Julia Charles
Creative Director Leslie
  Harrington
Prop Stylists Jo Harris and
  Liz Belton
Food Stylist Lucy Williams
Indexer Hilary Bird

First published in 2013 and 2017
as *The Vegan Baker*

This edition published in 2024
by Ryland Peters & Small
20–21 Jockey's Fields
London WC1R 4BW
and 341 E 116th St,
New York NY 10029

www.rylandpeters.com

10 9 8 7 6 5 4 3 2 1

Text © Dunja Gulin 2013, 2017
and 2024
Design and photographs
© Ryland Peters & Small 2013,
2017 and 2024

ISBN: 978-1-78879-597-5

A CIP record for this book is
available from the British Library.
US Library of Congress
Cataloging-in-Publication Data
has been applied for.

Printed in China

FSC
www.fsc.org
MIX
Paper | Supporting
responsible forestry
FSC® C008047

Notes

• Both British (Metric) and American (Imperial plus US cup) measurements are included in these recipes for your convenience, however it is important to work with one set of measurements only and not alternate between the two within a recipe. Liquid measurements listed in ounces should be considered fluid ounces. All spoon measurements are level unless otherwise specified. A teaspoon is 5 ml and a tablespoon is 15 ml.

• Ovens should be preheated to the specified temperature. If using a fan-assisted oven, adjust temperatures accordingly.

Contents

Introduction   6

Basics   8

1 SIMPLE CAKES & MUFFINS   22

2 FANCY CAKES   40

3 SLICES & BARS   56

4 COOKIES & BISCUITS   72

5 PIES, TARTS & STRUDELS   90

6 BREAD & SAVOURY BAKING   110

7 SPECIAL BAKED TREATS   130

Index   142

Acknowledgements   144

Introduction

Baking: it has always been a magical word for me. Sweet baking was, and still is, even more magical, and I think many people will understand what I'm saying! The smell of freshly baked crescent rolls my nonna used to make for Christmas is one of the few things I can remember from my early childhood.

Maybe that's why my first attempts in the kitchen were baking simple cakes, learning how to flip pancakes and burning batch after batch of cookies. But I never gave up.

At high school, I decided to stop eating meat, and later when I left home to study I decided to try eating more vegan food after sampling so many of the disastrous 'vegetarian' dishes we were offered in student canteens. Back then, finding a vegan dessert that wasn't either a brick or a mass of soggy gruel was next to impossible, especially on a student budget. Also, I adored desserts and had no intention of giving them up! So, I decided to take my sweet-tooth destiny into my own hands and start some serious vegan baking!

It wasn't easy. Like everything else in life, you have to work hard. As with most 'conventional baking', vegan baking has quite a lot of specific rules that you have to follow without exception. I feel that, in some cases, it has more in common with chemistry than it does with intuitive cooking! But, what I love about it is the unpredictability, the excitement, the anticipation and the burst of joy that one feels when an experiment bakes into a tasty and beautiful thing! And I'm lucky enough to have the opportunity to share some of my discoveries with the world. I feel honoured.

There are various possible reasons why you decided to give this book a try. You might be fed up with the heavy feeling in your stomach after eating a regular dessert. You might be allergic to dairy or eggs but don't want to miss out on eating tasty desserts. You could be vegan for ethical reasons and your new year's resolution is to test your talent in baking. Maybe you want to lose weight, or you might just be curious to

see how on earth you can bake a delicious dessert with 'nothing'…

Well, let me tell you, this 'nothing' that I use in making cakes are actually so many, so delicious and so healthy that the list will leave you speechless!

The reason I would encourage every person on this planet – whether vegan or not – to enjoy vegan desserts is the feeling you have after eating a healthy, natural dish that is not loaded with eggs, milk and sugar. Even though I don't have anything against these ingredients being eaten occasionally (in fact I do object to milk and sugar, but that's another story), when they are combined in a single dish, and especially when refined flour is used as well, they are quite harmful to the body, and can result in health problems in the long term.

However, taking any regime to extremes, vegan included, won't do much good for your health or

mental wellbeing. What I've noticed is that many vegan baking books are guided by one rule – all the recipes have to be vegan. That means they are still full of refined sugar, margarine, highly refined flour and other processed vegan ingredients. So, you opt for not eating any animal products, but you might also put yourself on the path to becoming an unhealthy vegan.

That is why, when testing baking recipes, I am guided by more rules than one. I want my vegan cakes to be healthy; I want them to be made with the best ingredients I can afford; I want them to be organic whenever possible; sweet but not overly sweet; visually appealing but not fussy; perfect in their imperfections; I want them to feed my body; and I want them to feed my soul. These are my eight golden rules. If most of them are met, the result will be a gorgeous homemade cake that no one will ever say 'no' to. Try and you'll see!

Now let's look at the ingredients used in healthy vegan baking, my way.

Essential vegan baking ingredients

FLOURS

As the essential ingredient in baking, flour makes a big difference in successful dessert-making so carefully choose the best kind available. Buy organic brands that are unbleached and not treated with chemicals. Store them in airtight containers to prevent bugs and moths having a feast. Do not substitute plain/all-purpose flour for wholemeal/whole-wheat flour if not stated in the recipe, as the latter has more bran and is heavier both in structure and taste. Quality and protein percentages vary from brand to brand and from season to season. This might result in baking problems and, even if the recipe works really well once, there is no guarantee it will work so well next time if you are using a different brand of flour. Don't get scared! I'll talk more about this in the troubleshooting section on pages 16–17.

Unbleached plain/all-purpose flour

I use this type of flour most often since it makes a great base for almost any flour combination, and I would recommend using at least 60% of this type of flour in cake mixtures and bread dough to get a good texture and rise. It can be replaced with unbleached spelt flour if you prefer spelt to wheat. In emergencies, you can use bleached flour instead.

Wholemeal/whole-wheat flour

Robust and full-flavoured, wholemeal/whole-wheat flour contains – besides starch and protein – vitamins, fibre and minerals from the wheat's bran and germ. It has a shorter shelf-life, which is a good sign, but moths love it, so keep it tightly stored. If you live in a hot climate, keep it refrigerated. In baking, using entirely wholemeal/whole-wheat flour usually results in a heavy, dense and nutty texture and flavour which isn't usually what we want for a cake. A small percentage (up to 15%) added to the unbleached flour, however, will give a great texture and add flavour to any cake mixture or dough.

Fine cornmeal

There seems to be some confusion between the terms cornflour, cornmeal and cornstarch in British and American English. By cornmeal I mean yellow flour made out of dried corn kernels that is finely ground and used in baking, mixed with other flours. It should not be very coarse (like polenta) and it should not be a completely white powder (like cornflour/cornstarch). Cornmeal is quite heavy and dense, so I never use it on its own. It makes lovely sweet-tasting breads and gives a nice yellow colour to pie and tart crusts. Cornflour/cornstarch is used as a thickener (see page 15).

Other flours and grain products

There are always a couple more types of flour and grain products stored in my cupboard, waiting to be used. *Spelt flour* is nice to have for variety and when you wish to lessen the gluten content in baking. Sometimes a dough might ask for more protein, for example in bread, so having *strong/bread flour* is also good. *Chestnut flour* is a treat and I use it for special occasions to make delicious Castagnaccio (page 32). *Semolina/farina* is a type of ground wheat, completely white and mostly used to make semolina pudding, not as a flour. But I found some interesting ways for using it in baking and I hope you will like the taste and texture of those desserts as much as I do! *Couscous* is also a wheat product, more coarsely ground than semolina, and yellowish in colour. It gives a great crunch to cookies!

Filo/phyllo pastry are paper-thin sheets made out of flour and water and used for making all kinds of baked delicacies, especially in Middle Eastern and Balkan cuisines. My baking is somewhat influenced by the latter, so you will find a couple of interesting, exotic and very tasty desserts made with this dough. Don't be afraid of it and try each filo/phyllo recipe at least once – you'll be surprised how tasty and easy they are!

Clockwise from top left:
Chestnut flour, wholemeal/whole-wheat flour, unbleached plain/all-purpose flour, couscous, cornmeal

Left to right:
Agave syrup,
maple syrup,
brown rice syrup,
barley malt,
Demerara sugar

SWEETENERS

How to make desserts sweet and still be classed as healthy is one of the great mysteries. It can be done, but any answer I or some other cookbook author offers will probably be a potential topic for debate. What I have realized is that, especially in the United States, one healthy sweetener takes the throne and is revered until a controversy breaks out and another, 'healthier' sweetener takes the stage, then another and so on. In my opinion, the truth lies somewhere in between.

We all know processed foods are not good for us. At all. White sugar is one of the most refined foods available, and I never ever use it in my kitchen and avoid eating any food that contains it. This is not easy, as processed sugar is hiding everywhere; peeping from every can, every jar and every bread basket!

The sweeteners that I'm suggesting are the ones available to me and those that I have tested over the years, paying attention to how I felt after eating desserts sweetened with these rather than highly refined sugar. I have become quite sensitive to refined sugar over time and feel hot, restless and unfocussed when I eat it. I encourage you to test my method and see the difference for yourself: stop eating anything with refined sugar for a period of 30 days and then 'treat' yourself with a piece of your usual sugary cake. You should notice the bitter taste that sugary creams have and how afterwards your mouth feels weird and you need to brush your teeth immediately. For me, sugar acts like a mild poison, and I feel happy to have realized that early

enough in life to stop my sugar addiction. That's right, eating sugar becomes an addiction; it's a relatively new addiction that is socially acceptable and encouraged by the media. It's a gazillion-dollar business that throws people into diabetes, obesity, high blood-pressure problems and nervous breakdowns. It makes children irritable, hyperactive and naughty. It is slowly destroying our bodies by 'eating' all the calcium we get from other foods, causing osteoporosis on all seven continents. If these facts shock you, it's a good start. Maybe I will reach some of you and you'll think over your daily abuse of sugar and try to make changes in your diet.

I don't want to induce a fear of any food, not even sugar. It will not harm you if you have a piece of cake with sugar once a month, but if you have a cup of coffee with sugar in it for breakfast, eat a sandwich with white bread for lunch, drink two cups of juice during the day, and cook pasta with canned tomato sauce for dinner, it's likely that you are eating too much of it. And that's without even having a sweet treat!

Having said this, I do use some types of unrefined sugars if other sweeteners will not work as well. This is the case in cake frostings where finely ground, unrefined Demerara sugar replaces icing/confectioners' sugar to make a fluffy buttercream. It cannot be done with rice or agave syrup. Or, for example, in some cookie recipes, where I want a crunchy texture that cannot be achieved with liquid sweeteners. Also, unrefined sugars taste sweeter

than liquid sweeteners, so if I'm making a cocoa cake mixture, I need more sweetness to make up for the bitterness of the cocoa powder.

Apart from these mentioned cases, if you wish to swap one sweetener stated in a recipe for another, feel free to do so and see what happens. Many vegan recipes warn you that other liquid contents in the recipe have to be reduced if you decide to use rice syrup instead of sugar. I don't think that is true. I have made cake after cake where I have swapped the sugar for brown rice syrup and not changed anything else, and they always came out great. But if it doesn't work for you, there might be other factors at play. I'll discuss that in the troubleshooting section on pages 16–17.

Brown rice syrup

I consider brown rice syrup to be the best choice out of all existing sweeteners. Maybe it's because of my background as a macrobiotic chef, but it might also be that it really is the best! Desserts made with it always have a mild taste and are soothing and comforting as opposed to the aggressive taste of conventional sweets. However, there are rice syrups and rice syrups on the market, so to make your shopping easier, here are a few guidelines on how to recognize a good one.

The highest-quality brands of rice syrup (sometimes called rice malt syrup) are traditionally made by a slow, natural enzymatic process out of whole grains. The complex carbohydrates that rice syrup consists of are slowly digested and provide us with stable energy instead of being absorbed immediately and causing rapid surges in blood sugar levels.

Read the labels. If sprouted barley is among the ingredients, the syrup can be used daily. Being thick, somewhat darker and of a slightly distinctive taste, it might not work in every recipe, so have a jar of light brown rice syrup in your kitchen as well. Just be careful to buy organic brands that do not have sugar listed as one of the ingredients!

Barley malt

This is a high-quality sweetener you will find in only one or two recipes in this book, as it has quite a strong taste and is too heavy to be used in desserts you might want to offer to wide audiences. But it's good to have it around and use it in teas, healing hot lemonades, porridges or when making Grissini with Caraway Seeds (see page 120)! It can also be used in pie or cookie doughs, if you don't mind its taste and the dark colour of the resultant baked goodies.

Pure maple syrup

Maple syrup is another good-quality sweetener that, apart from tasting sweet, is rich in trace minerals which act as antioxidants, keep your heart healthy and support your immune system. When shopping for maple syrup, search for pure and organic types that are dark in colour. Make sure there is no added sugar or colouring in the ingredients. I use it in richer cake mixtures and in nut-rich desserts, as well as in many cookie recipes. It gives a deep and rich taste.

Corn and tofu pie
*Made with olive oil and soy milk in
place of butter and cows' milk*

Agave syrup (or nectar)

A highly controversial sweetener, this has been glorified and frowned upon over and over in the past couple of years. Its visual similarity to honey, its strong, sweet taste and its availability in many food stores has made it quite popular and widely used. It is high in fructose and is quite processed but sometimes you have to make a choice between a bad sweetener (refined sugar) and one that is better, but not ideal at all (in this case, agave syrup). I would put rice and maple syrup highly above it, quality-wise, but if you're in good health, occasional use should not do much harm. Overuse, however, could. Feel free to substitute it with brown rice or maple syrup in each and every one of my recipes. Sometimes its strong, sweet taste is necessary, but if the dessert is slightly less sweet, it's not the end of the world. I don't want to judge agave syrup, but it's important to know the facts and make informed choices. I feel fine using it from time to time but I use the other sweeteners listed much more often.

Unrefined sugars

In cases where there is no substitution possible (as mentioned on page 10), I try to find the best-quality, organic, unrefined sugar that will work well in a specific vegan baking recipe. You might have a better choice, so pick the best one you can. I use Demerara, muscovado and sometimes, if I can get hold of it, sucanat (whole cane sugar). Sugar is sugar, but the unrefined varieties are more wholesome than the highly processed ones, containing minerals and trace elements and taking a little longer to digest.

OILS

Oils play an important role in baking but I use them in smaller amounts than most vegan baking recipes ask for. It's good to think about the dessert you're going to make first and then choose which oil to use, as some oils carry a strong taste that might interfere with other ingredients. Organic, cold-pressed oils are my preferred choice, and even though they are more expensive than highly refined oils, I try to save money on other things

and not on the quality of the oil I use daily! There are many other kinds of oil you could use apart from those listed below, depending on what is available to you.

Sunflower oil

Organic, cold-pressed sunflower oil for cooking and baking is an excellent choice that can be used in almost any baking recipe in this book, since it is odourless and mild. It is partially refined to remove the specific taste and smell of sunflower seeds, but being cold pressed makes it healthier than cheap, refined oil. I always have a stash of it in my kitchen as it's excellent for deep frying and sautéing as well.

Extra virgin olive oil

It is not surprising that I try to sneak in olive oil wherever I can; my Mediterranean blood is to blame, and my grandma supplying me with her own Istrian olive oil doesn't help either! I don't mind its slightly bitter taste and I use it in sweet baking a lot, even though this raises a few eyebrows at my baking workshops! Some people say that heat damages good-quality olive oil, and it probably does, but I eat enough of it uncooked, so I'm not afraid to sometimes bake a delicious cake, cookie or cracker with it!

Safflower oil

This oil is made from safflower seeds and is nutritionally similar to sunflower oil. It is high in monounsaturated fats and lower in saturates than olive oil, which makes it quite appealing for healthfood enthusiasts. Another good quality of this oil is its high smoke point, which means it's suitable for high-heat cooking and baking.

Virgin coconut oil

Coconut oil has received much attention and made a big comeback in cooking and baking in the past couple of years. For a long time, it was considered a source of saturated fats which were deemed bad, and this is still true for hydrogenated coconut oil. But today, it is known that some types of saturated fats are good for you and that virgin coconut oil mostly contains healthy fats. It solidifies at lower

temperatures so I like to use it instead of margarine in recipes, even though this only works in some cases. It's also delicious!

Non-hydrogenated margarine

I try to avoid using margarine often and in large amounts, and this goes for healthier, non-hydrogenated margarine too. However, some recipes really call for it and we would never have fluffy vegan 'buttercreams' and frostings on cakes and cupcakes were it not for margarine. So, a couple of times a year I make my husband and my guests happy by making layer cakes that resemble conventional cakes so much that no one would ever notice they were made without eggs, refined sugar and dairy!

NON-DAIRY MILKS

There is a wide choice of non-dairy milks nowadays, but each type behaves differently in vegan baking recipes. Here are some tips for success in making cakes and cookies that might help you to avoid baking disasters!

Organic, non-gmo, plain soy milk

This is the best liquid for vegan baking as it contains the most protein of all plant milks and is the best alternative to cow's milk in baking, especially in cake mixtures. If it can be replaced by another non-dairy milk, it will be stated in the recipe. Sometimes soy milk may be substituted for soy yogurt. Buy unflavoured, unsweetened milk unless otherwise stated in the recipe.

Coconut milk

This is thick and creamy in texture and has a coconut flavour that works well in some recipes for cake and cookie mixtures. In my opinion, it is more suitable for daily use for people living in a hot climate, but occasional use in baking is a good and tasty change from other non-dairy milks.

Oat milk

This is naturally sweet and works well in frostings and cake creams. It can be combined with soy milk in cake mixtures to give extra moisture but do not add too much as it can cause the cake to crumble.

Top to bottom:
Soy milk, rice milk, coconut milk

Rice milk

Although lovely and sweet, this is quite watery and contains almost no protein, which is required for good vegan baking. It can be used in some cookies, especially with ground flaxseeds which contribute fat and bulk.

Other plant-based milks

Nut and seed milks can work in some vegan baking recipes but may change the texture, taste or consistency, especially in cakes. I would suggest using them for cake creams and frostings rather than in sensitive cake recipes, particularly if you are not an experienced vegan baker.

RAISING AGENTS

Smart use of raising agents is what makes the difference between a heavy cake and a fluffy and light one! I have noticed that many people overuse raising agents in vegan baking to make sure the mixture rises. It's not about quantity but about mixing the best combination to achieve consistent rising results, ie. bicarbonate of/baking soda, baking powder and a little vinegar or lemon juice always results in pure fluffiness!

Aluminium-free baking powder

This has the same rising properties as commercial baking powder, only it's better for you! Also, the flavour of your baked goods will improve substantially as aluminium gives a bitter aftertaste.

Bicarbonate of/baking soda

This is important in vegan baking as it gives that extra 'push' to cake mixtures that might otherwise turn out heavy and dense. It reacts with acidic ingredients and that's why you'll find vinegar, lemon juice, soy yogurt or cocoa alongside it in every recipe of mine.

Active dry yeast (emulsifier-free)

This type of yeast is convenient for long-term storage and must be rehydrated before use. It is sensitive to temperature changes, so avoid exposing the dough to draughts while it is rising.

THICKENERS

Of all three thickeners given here, agar is the star and far superior to animal gelatine.

Agar

This natural vegetable gelatine is derived from a red sea vegetable. It is unflavoured, rich in minerals and fibre, and calorie-free. It aids digestion and weight loss, so you could actually be eating a delicious dessert and helping your body to get rid of toxins – pure magic! I cannot understand why conventional dessert-makers do not switch from yucky gelatine (which is made out of pig skin, bovine hides and bones) to this beautiful plant gelatine that feeds you with minerals and makes your desserts delicious, all at the same time! However, it does not make liquids creamy, only firm. That's why, in my cream and frosting recipes, I mostly combine agar with a small amount of cornflour/cornstarch or arrowroot to add creaminess and get a firm texture.

Cornflour/cornstarch

Cornflour/cornstarch is a thickening agent which I use in creams, mousses and frostings, or in cake mixtures to make the cake more elastic and prevent crumbling. It is not the healthiest ingredient, but it is a faithful companion on your road to baking stardom! Try to buy organic, non-gmo cornflour/cornstarch. See also page 8.

Arrowroot powder

This healthy, natural thickener is used in the same way as cornflour/cornstarch but don't use too much of it when thickening creams as it can turn slimy! Heat it only until the mixture thickens, not longer, to prevent thinning. I encourage you to use it but it cannot always replace cornflour/cornstarch so stick to my recipe instructions.

Troubleshooting

Baking is lovely but quite unpredictable, and baking failures can be caused by so many external (and internal) factors, that even if you follow the same cake recipe to the letter, there's no guarantee it will come out the same way it did last time. Especially in vegan baking! It's good to be aware of this at the beginning of your baking adventures, otherwise you might end up throwing away all your baking cookbooks because you feel no baked goodie ever comes out as the recipe says or as it looks on the photo.

To help you out, here are a couple of things that might happen when you're baking, possible reasons why, and directions as to what to do next time you decide to dirty your bowls, spatulas and baking pans!

CAKE

Did not rise? A cake can turn out heavy and dense for many reasons: not sifting dry ingredients, overmixing, using ingredients and pans that are too cold, not preheating the oven, stale baking powder, too much wholemeal/whole-wheat flour compared to unbleached flour, or opening the oven for the first 15 minutes of baking. Maybe the flour used has a very low percentage of protein or you didn't add a crucial acidic ingredient to the batter (lemon, vinegar, etc.).

Sank after baking? Similar reasons to the above. Maybe you threw too many things in at the same time, or your baking pan was too deep and the mixture too liquidy.

Soggy and sticky? It hasn't baked long enough, there was too much liquid in the mixture, or some of the reasons stated in the first two paragraphs. Or you didn't wait for it to cool completely before cutting into it.

Bitter tasting? Too much baking powder that contains aluminium. Use aluminium-free baking powder and measure the amount stated in the recipe carefully.

Cupcake/muffin mixture stuck to the paper cases? You didn't wait long enough for them to cool! Or they are under-baked because your oven is lazy. Buy a good oven thermometer and remember to bake them for longer next time.

PIE AND TART CRUST

Too crumbly to shape? Not enough water. Add a few drops at a time, or just press the dough into the pan without adding any water. Even though it's crumbly, it can result in a good crust because it expands and binds together during baking.

Hard? Definitely overbaked. Maybe you kneaded it too vigorously and for too long, and pie dough hates that. Next time, knead it gently and just enough for the ingredients to come together.

Sticky and oily? It's crucial that the water, flour and margarine are chilled before use, and if they get too warm from the temperature of the kitchen or your warm hands, the oil from the margarine will separate during baking and render an oily and crumbly dough that is impossible to slice.

Soggy bottom? If you are making a pie with a wet filling (like apple pie, etc.) the bottom crust needs to be blind-baked for 7–10 minutes before you fill it. If that isn't done, the bottom crust will not get enough heat and the fruit juice will make it soggy.

COOKIES

Dry and hard? They've spent too much time in the oven! Put on a timer next time you bake them because a minute or two too long and they become brown rocks. Maybe there's too much flour in the dough. Did you forget to add the raising agent stated in the recipe?

Floppy instead of crunchy? This always happens if you decide to substitute the unrefined sugar asked for in the recipe with liquid sweetener such as rice syrup or agave. They will still taste great, but they will not be crunchy. Or maybe you stuck to the recipe but you didn't bake them enough, or the temperature was too low? It's important to have a good oven thermometer.

Sticky? Under-baked. Or did you maybe accidentally add too much liquid?

PIZZA AND FOCACCIA, BEFORE BAKING

Didn't rise? Some of the reasons could be: the water used to activate the yeast was too cold, or it was too hot and killed the yeast; too much flour used; you didn't knead the dough long enough; the place where the dough was rising was too cool or draughty, or too hot (yeast killed again). Maybe the flour used does not have a high enough percentage of protein, or you left the dough to rise for too long?

Sticky after rising? Too much liquid or not enough flour used, or you didn't knead it long enough.

YEAST DOUGH (AND NO-KNEAD BREAD DOUGH), AFTER BAKING

Pale? Didn't rise long enough before baking. Oven temperature was too low, or the bread is under-baked. Overcrowding the oven might also be a reason for this.

Uneven colour? Your oven is unreliable! Or did you put the bread in the corner, not the middle of the oven?

Heavy, dense and sticky? The yeast was not properly activated or it is stale. The dough was not kneaded long enough, or there was too much flour. Did you forget to take it out of the baking pan after baking and let it cool on a wire rack as stated in the recipe? Did you try to cut into it before it had cooled down completely?

CREAMS AND FROSTINGS

Cream didn't set? Not enough agar or uncooked agar. Maybe you didn't leave it to cool in the fridge long enough before slicing. Maybe you substituted soy milk or oat milk for rice milk, which is too watery. Over-cooking arrowroot powder also thins down the cream.

Cream is too hard? Too much agar. It happens often as agar does not thicken the cream while it's

hot, so people have a tendency to add more to make sure. Don't do that – trust the recipe. Also, be aware of whether you're using agar powder or flakes, as powder is much stronger and you need to use less of it (1 teaspoon agar powder to 1–2 tablespoons flakes).

Cream is floury? Too much cornflour/cornstarch added, or it was not cooked for long enough.

Cream is lumpy? Either you didn't dilute the thickener at all before adding it to the cream, or you diluted it in warm water and got a lumpy mess. Or you did everything properly, but while pouring it into the hot cream you didn't whisk vigorously enough and the heat was too fierce?

Cream is slimy? Too much arrowroot powder added.

Frosting not fluffy? The margarine was at the wrong temperature – it has to be room temperature, but not too soft and oily. Maybe you didn't sift in the cocoa and sugar, or you added cold liquid into it while creaming.

Chocolate seized/split while melting over a pan of simmering water? Heat is too high, the heatproof bowl is touching the water underneath (don't let it!), you were not stirring continuously or a drop of water found its way into the melting chocolate. Dry the bowl and the whisk/spatula really well and do not cover the chocolate with a lid while it's melting.

FILO/PHYLLO PASTRY

Cracked while making strudel? The sheets were left uncovered and dried out. Keep them covered with a damp kitchen towel while you assemble the strudel, and if you have leftover sheets, keep them in the fridge wrapped in clingfilm/plastic wrap or in a sealed bag.

Cracked after baking? Cover the strudel with a dry kitchen towel after baking and allow to cool. This will loosen up the crust. It's a good idea to score the strudel with a sharp knife before baking to mark the place where you want to slice it after baking. This will make your slices neat and the crust will remain undamaged.

Basic chocolate cake

FOR A 23-CM/9-IN. CAKE

300 ml/1⅓ cups plain soy milk
⅔ teaspoon apple cider vinegar
180 g/1⅓ cups unbleached plain/all-purpose flour
⅔ teaspoon bicarbonate of/baking soda
⅔ teaspoon baking powder
40 g/½ cup cocoa powder
a pinch of salt
40 g/⅓ cup plain wholemeal/whole-wheat flour
a pinch of ground cinnamon
120 g/½ cup pure maple syrup
70 g/⅓ cup sunflower or safflower oil
grated zest of 1 orange or lemon
80 g/4 tablespoons fruit jam
2 teaspoons rum or juice of ½ orange or lemon

23-cm/9-in. springform cake pan, baselined with parchment paper and oiled

Makes 8–12 slices

FOR A 28-CM/11-IN. CAKE

450 ml/2 cups plain soy milk
1 teaspoon apple cider vinegar
260 g/2 cups unbleached plain/all-purpose flour
1 teaspoon bicarbonate of/baking soda
1 teaspoon baking powder
60 g/⅔ cup cocoa powder
¼ teaspoon salt
60 g/½ cup plain wholemeal/whole-wheat flour
¼ teaspoon ground cinnamon
170 g/⅔ cup pure maple syrup
100 g/½ cup sunflower or safflower oil
grated zest of 1 orange or lemon
125 g/6 tablespoons fruit jam
2 teaspoons rum or juice of ½ orange or lemon

28-cm/11-in. springform cake pan, baselined with parchment paper and oiled

Makes 12–15 slices

Preheat the oven to 180°C (350°F) Gas 4.

Mix together the milk and vinegar in a bowl and set aside for 10 minutes.

Sift the unbleached flour, bicarbonate of/baking soda, baking powder, cocoa and salt into a mixing bowl, then add the wholemeal/whole-wheat flour and cinnamon and mix well.

Add the syrup*, oil and zest to the vinegar mixture and mix well. Gently fold these into the dry ingredients with a spatula. Make sure not to mix too much, otherwise the cake might turn chewy. When everything is just incorporated, spoon the mixture into the prepared cake pan and spread evenly with the spatula.

Bake in the preheated oven for 20–25 minutes or until a skewer inserted in the middle comes out clean. Spring open the cake pan and allow the cake to cool completely.

When the cake is cold, peel off the paper. Slice the cake in half horizontally with a large, serrated knife. You can also cut off the top if it has domed while baking and you prefer it to be flat.

Put the jam and rum or juice in a small saucepan and heat until it comes to the boil. Spread this over both cake layers – this will make the cake moist and stop any frosting from seeping into the cake. Allow to cool.

Put the lower cake layer back in the cake pan and attach the springform ring. The cake is now ready to be topped or filled.

*If you are serving the cake as it is (without a filling or frosting), add a little extra syrup to the mixture, or spread something sweet over the cake after baking.

For a 23-cm/9-in. cake

360 ml/1⅔ cups plain soy milk

⅔ teaspoon apple cider vinegar

50 g/¾ cup ground nuts, 50 g/½ cup whole nuts, or 40 g/⅔ cup desiccated coconut

170 g/1⅓ cups unbleached plain/all-purpose flour

¾ teaspoon bicarbonate of/baking soda

1¼ teaspoons baking powder

30 g/2½ tablespoons cornflour/cornstarch

¼ teaspoon bourbon vanilla powder or ½ teaspoon vanilla extract

a pinch of salt

50 g/⅓ cup plain wholemeal/whole-wheat flour

2½ teaspoons ground flaxseeds

80 g/⅓ cup sunflower or safflower oil

130 g/½ cup brown rice syrup

100 g/5 tablespoons fruit jam

2 teaspoons rum or water

23-cm/9-in. springform cake pan, baselined with parchment paper and oiled

Makes 8–12 slices

For a 28-cm/11-in. cake

450 ml/2 cups plain soy milk

1 teaspoon apple cider vinegar

60 g/1 cup ground nuts, 60 g/½ cup whole nuts, or 50 g/⅔ cup desiccated coconut

210 g/1⅔ cups unbleached plain/all-purpose flour

1 teaspoon bicarbonate of/baking soda

1½ teaspoons baking powder

40 g/3 tablespoons cornflour/cornstarch

¼ teaspoon bourbon vanilla powder or ½ teaspoon vanilla extract

¼ teaspoon salt

60 g/½ cup plain wholemeal/whole-wheat flour

1 tablespoon ground flaxseeds

100 g/½ cup sunflower or safflower oil

160 g/⅔ cup brown rice syrup

125 g/6 tablespoons fruit jam

2 teaspoons rum or water

28-cm/11-in. springform cake pan, baselined with parchment paper and oiled

Makes 12–15 slices

Basic nut cake

Preheat the oven to 180°C (350°F) Gas 4.

Mix together the milk and vinegar in a bowl and set aside for 10 minutes.

If you are using whole nuts, grind them finely using a spice mill or food processor.

Sift the unbleached flour, bicarbonate of/baking soda, baking powder, cornflour/cornstarch, vanilla and salt into a mixing bowl, add the nuts, wholemeal/whole-wheat flour and flaxseeds and mix well.

Add the oil and syrup* to the vinegar mixture and mix well. Gently fold these into the dry ingredients with a spatula. Do not mix too much, otherwise the cake might turn chewy. When everything is just incorporated, spoon the mixture into the prepared cake pan and spread evenly with the spatula.

Bake in the preheated oven for 20–25 minutes or until a skewer inserted in the middle comes out clean. Spring open the cake pan and allow the cake to cool completely.

When the cake is cold, peel off the paper. Slice the cake in half horizontally with a large, serrated knife. You can also cut off the top if it has domed while baking and you prefer it to be flat.

Put the jam and rum or juice in a small saucepan and heat until it comes to the boil. Spread this over both cake layers – this will make the cake moist and stop any frosting from seeping into the cake. Allow to cool.

Put the lower cake layer back in the cake pan and attach the springform ring. The cake is now ready to be topped or filled.

*If you are serving the cake as it is (without a filling or frosting), add a little extra syrup to the mixture, or spread something sweet over the cake after baking.

Sweet pie dough

400 g/3 cups unbleached plain/all-purpose flour

150 g/1 cup fine cornmeal

3 teaspoons baking powder

½ teaspoon salt

240 g/2 cups non-hydrogenated margarine, chilled

130 g/½ cup brown rice or agave syrup

grated zest of 1 lemon

70–110 ml/⅓–½ cup ice-cold water

40 x 28-cm/16 x 11-in. baking pan (for a thinner crust) or 23 x 30 cm/9 x 12-in. baking pan (for a thicker crust)

Put the flour, cornmeal, salt and baking powder in a food processor and pulse to mix. Add the margarine and pulse 6–8 times until the mixture resembles coarse breadcrumbs. Add the syrup and lemon zest and pulse again a couple of times. Add ice-cold water one tablespoon at a time, pulsing until the mixture just begins to clump together. If you pinch some of the crumbly dough and it holds together, it's ready. If it doesn't, add a little more water and pulse again. Do not add too much water otherwise it will make the dough tough.

Place the dough on a lightly floured work surface. Knead it just enough to form a ball but do not over-knead it. Shape it into a disc, wrap it in clingfilm/plastic wrap and refrigerate it for at least 1 hour, and up to 2 days. If you're in a hurry you can chill the dough in the freezer for 15 minutes. If refrigerated, allow the dough to rest at room temperature for 5–10 minutes before rolling it out.

Preheat the oven to 180°C (350°F) Gas 4 and continue with the relevant recipe.

Pizza and focaccia dough

FOR THE STARTER

40 g/¼ cup rye flour

55 ml/¼ cup lukewarm water

9 g/2 teaspoons active dry yeast (additive-free)

FOR THE DOUGH

200 g/1½ cups unbleached spelt flour

30 g/¼ cup strong wholemeal/whole-wheat bread flour

½ teaspoon salt

110 ml/½ cup lukewarm water

1 tablespoon olive oil, plus extra for oiling

1 tablespoon soy milk

40 x 28-cm/16 x 11-in. baking pan (for pizza) or 23 x 30 cm/9 x 12-in. baking pan (for focaccia), well oiled

Mix together the starter ingredients in a mixing bowl, cover and allow to rest for 30 minutes.

For the dough, mix together the flours and salt in a bowl. Mix together the water, oil and milk in a jug, then add to the starter and mix well. Finally, add the dry ingredients to the mixing bowl and mix with a wooden spoon. Place the dough on a lightly floured work surface and knead for 5 minutes or until it is soft and slightly sticky. Add flour as you knead, but not more than necessary. Put the dough in a large, oiled bowl and rub a little oil on the surface of the dough, too. Cover the bowl with a clean, damp towel and allow to rise for 2½ hours in a warm place.

If making pizza, punch the dough down, cover and allow to rise for another 45 minutes. You can pretend to be a real pizzaiolo and stretch the dough with your hands, or use a rolling pin to flatten it to the size of the prepared baking pan. Sprinkle your chosen toppings over it and bake in an oven preheated to 200°C (400°F) Gas 6 for 15–20 minutes.

If making focaccia, shape the dough to fit the prepared baking pan by gently pressing and pushing it from the middle toward the edges. Make

Top and bottom:
*Pizza and focaccia dough;
sweet pie dough*

dimples by poking the dough with
your fingertips. Drizzle with olive oil,
cover and allow to rise again for 2 hours.

Sprinkle your chosen seasonings over the
dough. Bake in an oven preheated to 180°C
(350°F) Gas 4 for 20 minutes, or until golden
and crisp.

CHAPTER 1

Simple cakes and muffins

Breakfast, mid-morning, teatime or for a friend – there are so many occasions suited to simple cakes and muffins. With a gentle emphasis on fresh and dried fruits, nuts and seeds like quinoa, these are recipes to make and eat without guilt or moderation. They will satisfy a sweet craving while giving you a sustained supply of energy.

Muffins CAN be healthy, and full of nutritious ingredients and fibre! Actually, these are perfect for breakfast and are a good substitute for jam on toast when you don't have the time to sit down. Make them the night before, sleep 20 minutes longer in the morning and munch on them on your way to work!

Breakfast muffins with apples and jam

200 g/1½ cups unbleached plain/all-purpose flour

60 g/½ cup plain wholemeal/whole-wheat flour

2½ teaspoons baking powder

¼ teaspoon salt

½ teaspoon ground cinnamon

300 ml/1¼ cups plain soy milk

130 g/½ cup brown rice syrup

100 g/½ cup safflower or coconut oil

freshly squeezed juice and grated zest of 1 lemon

1 small apple, peeled, cored and diced

60 g/½ cup raisins

100 g/4 tablespoons firm apricot jam (or other)

12-hole muffin pan lined with paper cases

Makes 9–12

Preheat the oven to 180°C (350°F) Gas 4.

Sift together the flours, baking powder, salt and cinnamon in a bowl and mix well.

In a separate bowl, mix together the milk, syrup, oil, lemon juice and zest.

Combine both bowls and mix gently with a silicone spatula. Do not overmix otherwise the muffins will be tough. Add the apples and raisins and gently mix in.

Fill 9 of the muffin cases half-full with the mixture, then put 1 full teaspoon of jam on top. Cover each one with more of the cake mixture, making sure you fill the cases only three-quarters full. If you have any cake mixture left, repeat this process in further muffin cases until you run out of mixture.

Bake in the preheated oven for 30 minutes or until golden.

Remove from the muffin pan and allow to cool on a wire rack.

Marble cake, marble squares, marble bundt cake – I've been chased by marbled desserts all my life, since every family around me has its own special recipe for this light-dark cake creation. So I made myself a promise that one day I, too, would have my own special marbled dessert recipe! And here it is, in the shape of these wonderfully moist, banana-and-cocoa-flavoured muffins. Try to use coconut milk, as I suggest, as it gives a special consistency to the mixture, although using more soy milk would also work. The same goes for the cocoa nibs which can be replaced by an additional 1½ tablespoons cocoa powder, but freshly ground nibs will give you an energy kick!

Marbled energy muffins

1 tablespoon raw cocoa nibs

130 g/1 cup unbleached plain/ all-purpose flour

60 g/½ cup plain wholemeal/ whole-wheat flour

¼ teaspoon bourbon vanilla powder

1 teaspoon baking powder

½ teaspoon bicarbonate of/ baking soda

¼ teaspoon salt

100 g/½ cup coconut oil

110 ml/½ cup coconut milk

170 ml/¾ cup plain soy milk

½ teaspoon apple cider vinegar

170 g/⅔ cup pure maple syrup

1 ripe banana

¼ teaspoon pure almond extract (optional)

grated zest of 1 lemon

1 tablespoon raw cocoa powder

12-hole muffin pan lined with paper cases

Makes 10–12

Preheat the oven to 180°C (350°F) Gas 4.

In a coffee or spice grinder, grind the cocoa nibs to a coarse powder.

Sift together the flours, vanilla powder, baking powder, bicarbonate of/ baking soda and salt in a bowl and mix well.

If the coconut oil has solidified, put the jar in a bowl of hot water until the oil has softened. Put the coconut oil, milks, vinegar, syrup, banana, almond extract, if using, and lemon zest in a food processor and blend until smooth.

Combine the dry and liquid ingredients, and mix gently with a silicone spatula. Spoon one third of the mixture into a separate bowl and fold in the ground cocoa nibs and cocoa powder.

Divide the plain cake mixture between 10–12 muffin cases. Put a spoonful of the cocoa mixture on top of that and, with the help of a chopstick or skewer, mix a little to get a marbled pattern.

Bake in the preheated oven for 18–20 minutes.

Remove from the muffin pan and allow to cool on a wire rack. This is a great picnic and lunchbox muffin!

This is a very simple recipe for muffins that are juicy, fruity and a little nutty too! Adding toasted wheat germ gives them a nice golden colour as well as providing a little extra taste, minerals, vitamins and fibre. Find it in your local healthfood store and use it not only in baking but also in cereals, salads and smoothies.

Summer muffins with raspberries and blackberries

325 g/2½ cups unbleached plain/all-purpose flour

65 g/½ cup plain wholemeal/whole-wheat flour

1½ teaspoons bicarbonate of/baking soda

1 teaspoon baking powder

¼ teaspoon salt

65 g/1 cup finely ground hazelnuts

25 g/3 tablespoons toasted wheat germ (optional)

420 ml/1¾ cups plain soy milk

200 g/¾ cup brown rice syrup

150 g/¾ cup sunflower oil

freshly squeezed juice of ½ lemon

100 g/1 small apple, peeled, cored and chopped

24 raspberries

24 blackberries

12-hole muffin pan lined with paper cases

Makes 12

Preheat the oven to 180°C (350°F) Gas 4.

Sift together the flours, bicarbonate of/baking soda, baking powder and salt in a bowl and add the ground hazelnuts and wheat germ, if using. Mix well.

Put the milk, syrup, oil, lemon juice and apple in a food processor and blend until smooth.

Combine the dry and liquid ingredients, and mix gently with a silicone spatula. Do not overmix otherwise the muffins will be tough.

Divide the cake mixture between the muffin cases. Gently press 2 raspberries and 2 blackberries into each muffin so that they are half-dipped in the mixture.

Bake in the preheated oven for 25–30 minutes.

Allow to cool in the muffin pan for a few minutes, then transfer to a wire rack to cool completely.

Enjoy the muffins on the beach, by the pool, on a picnic in the shade or wherever you like to spend sunny summer days!

It is an old tradition in Istria, Croatia, for wedding guests to bring a light pound cake (originally Italian) called 'pan di Spagna'. Each guest adds a unique touch to their cake with their choice of nuts, fruits and decoration. This is my vegan version of 'pan di Spagna', or if you like, 'pan d'Istria'!

Pan di Spagna

90 g/⅔ cup fine cornmeal

120 g/1 cup unbleached plain/ all-purpose flour

45 g/⅓ cup plain wholemeal/ whole-wheat flour

3 teaspoons baking powder

1 teaspoon bicarbonate of/ baking soda

¼ teaspoon salt

¼ teaspoon bourbon vanilla powder

60 g/½ cup pine nuts

40 g/¼ cup chopped walnuts

150 ml/⅔ cup plain soy milk

1 teaspoon apple cider vinegar

65 g/⅓ cup olive oil

85 g/⅓ cup brown rice or agave syrup

2 tablespoons Grappa (grape-based brandy), brandy or rum

grated zest and freshly squeezed juice of 1 lemon

90 g/⅔ cup chopped dried figs

finely ground unrefined sugar, for dusting

23-cm/9-in. springform cake pan, baselined with parchment paper and oiled

Serves about 10

Preheat the oven to 180°C (350°F) Gas 4.

Sift together the cornmeal, flours, baking powder, bicarbonate of/baking soda, salt and vanilla powder in a bowl and mix well. Add the pine nuts and walnuts and mix.

In a separate bowl, mix together the milk, vinegar, oil, syrup, alcohol, lemon juice and zest. Add the figs and incorporate well.

Combine both bowls and mix gently with a silicone spatula until well combined. Do not overmix otherwise the cake will be chewy and won't rise well.

Spoon the cake mixture into the prepared cake pan and spread level with the spatula. Bake in the preheated oven for 30–35 minutes.

Allow the cake to cool completely before removing it from the pan. If you wish, dust the top of the cold cake with a little finely ground unrefined sugar just before serving.

Castagnaccio, or chestnut cake, is a traditional Tuscan dessert and one of the few Italian desserts that doesn't require a lot of sugar and eggs! Since the Istrian peninsula is also rich in chestnut trees, I grew up eating many different chestnut-based dishes, both sweet and savoury. This cake is something in between; the chestnut flour gives it a mild sweet taste but since no other sweetener is used, it's not the typically sweet cake you might expect. However, it's still wonderfully simple and tasty – once a poor man's dessert, it's now a delicacy enjoyed by gourmets around the world! And totally vegan!

Castagnaccio

60 g/½ cup raisins

1 tablespoon rum

300 g/2⅓ cups chestnut flour

¼ teaspoon salt

¼ teaspoon bourbon vanilla powder

grated zest of 1 orange

50 g/¼ cup olive oil

450–625 ml/2–3 cups rice milk

60 g/⅓ cup pine nuts

60 g/⅓ cup chopped hazelnuts

needles pulled from 1 fresh rosemary sprig

whipped soy cream or agave syrup, to serve

24-cm/9½-in. springform cake pan, well oiled

Serves about 8

Soak the raisins in a bowl of the rum and 2 tablespoons hot water while you prepare the other ingredients.

Preheat the oven to 200°C (400°F) Gas 6.

Sift together the flour, salt, vanilla powder in a bowl, then mix in the orange zest and half of the oil. Slowly whisk in the milk, adding just enough to get a smooth, soft batter; it should be soft enough to fall from the whisk, but not too liquid.

Drain the soaked raisins and pat them dry, then add them to the cake mixture. Pour the mixture into the prepared cake pan until about 2 cm/¾ inch thick in the pan – shallower is fine but deeper could result in a soggy texture.

Sprinkle the pine nuts, hazelnuts and rosemary needles evenly over the top of the cake and press them in lightly. Drizzle some of the remaining olive oil over the top.

Bake in the preheated oven for 30–40 minutes, or until a thin, cracked crust has formed. The inside should still be soft and moist. Allow to cool completely in the pan.

Serve the cake with a dollop of whipped soy cream or a drizzle of agave syrup. It will keep for a couple of days in an airtight container.

I love the taste and texture of this cake and the addition of sweet potato adds extra vitamin A and fibre while making it visually interesting. I also like using pumpkin or rhubarb in the same way, when sweet potatoes aren't available.

Sweet potato pound cake

125 g/1 full cup peeled and cubed sweet potato

130 g/1 cup unbleached plain/all-purpose flour

65 g/½ cup plain wholemeal/whole-wheat flour

1 teaspoon bicarbonate of/baking soda

1 teaspoon baking powder

¼ teaspoon salt

100 g/½ cup raw/unrefined brown sugar

110 ml/½ cup sparkling mineral water

3 tablespoons apple concentrate (see method for an alternative)

65 g/⅓ cup sunflower oil

100 g/⅔ cup plain, soft tofu

100 ml/½ cup oat or soy cream

1-kg/2-lb. loaf pan, neatly lined with parchment paper (if you snip diagonally into the corners of the paper, it will fit more snugly into the pan)

Makes 8–10 slices

Preheat the oven to 180°C (350°F) Gas 4.

Steam the cubes of sweet potato for 10 minutes or until they are soft, but they should not fall apart when you prick them.

Sift together the flours, bicarbonate of/baking soda, baking powder and salt in a bowl and mix well.

Mix together the sparkling water and apple concentrate. You can use apple juice instead, but the sparkling water works well with bicarbonate of/baking soda and baking powder and makes this cake moist and spongy.

In a separate bowl, mix together the apple juice, oil, tofu and cream until smooth.

Combine the dry and liquid ingredients and mix until smooth. Fold in the steamed cubes of potato, reserving a couple of pieces for decoration.

Pour the mixture into the prepared loaf pan and spread level with a spatula. Sprinkle the reserved potatoes over the top and press them in lightly.

Bake the cake in the preheated oven for 25 minutes or until a skewer inserted in the middle comes out clean. Allow to cool in the pan for 10 minutes, then remove it, peel off the paper and allow to cool completely on a wire rack.

Serve a slice of the cake with a cup of warm green tea scented with lemon or lime. The best way to keep the cake moist is wrapped in a clean kitchen towel.

This is a recipe for (in my opinion) a healthy combination of ingredients which are transformed, with a little love and effort, into a very tasty loaf that will make the whole family happy. Not to mention the fact that many ingredients in this recipe can be replaced with any of the fruits, seeds and nuts that have been cluttering your kitchen cupboards for months!

Rich tea bread

60 g/½ cup dried plums
60 g/½ cup dates
40 g/⅓ cup dried cranberries
2 tablespoons dried goji berries
60 g/½ cup raisins
330 ml/1½ cups strong, hot tea
  (eg. rosehip and aniseed)
3 tablespoons brown rice or
  pure maple syrup
freshly squeezed juice and
  grated zest of 1 orange
65 g/⅓ cup sunflower oil
200 g/1½ cups flour (eg.
  unbleached spelt flour
  plus unbleached plain/
  all-purpose flour)
1 teaspoon baking powder
1 teaspoon bicarbonate of/
  baking soda
¼ teaspoon salt
½ teaspoon ground cinnamon
¼ teaspoon ground nutmeg
¼ teaspoon ground ginger
110 g/⅔ cup chopped cashews
110 g/⅔ cup chopped walnuts
3 tablespoons chopped
  hazelnuts or pine nuts

1-kg/2-lb. loaf pan, oiled

Makes 8–10 slices

Chop all the dried fruit into pieces roughly the same size as the raisins. Take the strong, hot tea and pour over the chopped fruit in a mixing bowl. Allow it to steep for at least 30 minutes or longer.

Preheat the oven to 180°C (350°F) Gas 4.

Add the syrup, orange juice and zest and the oil to the bowl of soaked fruit and mix well.

In a separate bowl, mix together the flour, baking powder, bicarbonate of/baking soda, salt, cinnamon, nutmeg, ginger, cashews, walnuts and hazelnuts or pine nuts. Add them to the fruit mixture and mix again with a wooden spoon until incorporated.

Spoon the cake mixture into the prepared loaf pan and spread level with a spatula. Bake in the preheated oven for 45–55 minutes or until a skewer inserted in the middle comes out clean. Allow to cool in the pan for 10 minutes, then remove and allow to cool completely on a wire rack.

Serve a slice of the cake with a cup of hot tea, of the same type used in the cake!

These are not just any scones; they are full of fibre and nutrients and totally sugar-free! Quinoa must be the most often used grain in my kitchen so I always have some leftovers in the fridge. One day I came up with a great way to use some of that by adding pre-cooked quinoa to my scone dough! A touch of dried fruit and agave syrup gives them a mild sweet taste, so you should top them with your favourite fruit jam if you're craving a sweet treat. These scones are a great breakfast, a great snack, great as travel food; actually they are great any time of the day, wherever you are!

Quinoa scones

5 tablespoons cooked quinoa (see method for an alternative)

130 g/1 cup unbleached plain/ all-purpose flour

60 g/½ cup plain wholemeal/ whole-wheat flour

2 teaspoons baking powder

½ teaspoon salt

45 g/¼ cup non-hydrogenated margarine, chilled

1 tablespoon coarse cornmeal/ polenta

110 ml/½ cup buttermilk (made from 110 ml/½ cup soy milk mixed with ½ teaspoon apple cider vinegar and left to rest for 5-10 minutes)

30 g/¼ cup dried fruit of your choice (raisins, dates, etc.)

3 tablespoons brown rice or agave syrup

baking sheet lined with parchment paper

Makes 10

If you want to cook the quinoa from scratch, boil 250 ml/1 cup water in a saucepan, then add 90 g/½ cup quinoa and a pinch of salt. Lower the heat and simmer for 20 minutes or until the quinoa has absorbed all the water. Allow the quinoa to cool.

Preheat the oven to 200°C (400°F) Gas 6.

Sift together the flours, baking powder and salt in a bowl. Add the margarine and rub it into the dry ingredients until the mixture resembles fine breadcrumbs. Stir in the quinoa and coarse cornmeal/polenta.

In a separate bowl, mix the buttermilk, dried fruit and syrup. Pour it into the dry ingredients and mix briefly with a spatula to a soft dough.

Divide the dough into 10 spoonfuls and drop onto the prepared baking sheet, leaving a little space between. Pat down the tops to neaten them.

Bake in the preheated oven for 15–20 minutes or until risen and golden. Allow to cool slightly on the baking sheet.

The scones are great served warm, fresh from the oven with a dollop of jam, but they are also yummy eaten cold, reheated in the oven, or toasted just before serving.

CHAPTER 2

Fancy cakes

For a birthday, special dinner, vegan tea party, Mother's Day, Father's Day and everything in between – this is your chance to pull out all the stops. These fancy cakes are layered, rich, show-stopping, and made with love. So set aside a bit of time, put your apron on, turn the radio up and enjoy baking a special cake for a special someone.

This is THE most popular cake of all the ones I make for both children's and grown-ups' birthdays! It's full of chocolate flavour, moist and very light. Don't tell your guests it's vegan and sugar-free, wait for their reaction, then confess! Nobody can ever tell this cake is super-healthy.

Chocolate layer cake

Basic Chocolate Cake (page 18, but see method here)

vegan chocolate shavings, to decorate

FOR THE CHOCOLATE CREAM

1.5 litres/6 cups chocolate soy or oat milk

195 g/¾ cup agave syrup

2 tablespoons cocoa powder

2½ teaspoons agar powder or 7 teaspoons agar flakes

3 tablespoons cornflour/cornstarch

100 g/scant ¾ cup finely chopped vegan dark/bittersweet chocolate (70% cocoa)

28-cm/11-in. or 23-cm/9-in. springform cake pan, baselined with parchment paper and oiled (see method)

Serves 8–15

For the Basic Chocolate Cake on page 18, decide which size you want to make before you start: a 23cm/9-in. cake for 8–12 slices or a 28-cm/11-in. cake for 12–15 slices, then follow the corresponding instructions. When you've baked the cake and prepared it as described on page 18, put the bottom layer back in the cake pan and set the top layer aside while you make the filling.

For the chocolate cream, put the milk and syrup in a large saucepan and add the cocoa powder and agar. Whisk and bring to the boil over medium heat. As soon as it comes to the boil, lower the heat before it bubbles over and makes a mess! Now boil gently for 4–5 minutes if you are using agar powder, or 10–12 minutes if you are using flakes or until the flakes have completely melted.

Mix the cornflour/cornstarch into 3 tablespoons cold water.

Add the chocolate to the hot cream, whisking vigorously until completely melted, then lower the heat to its lowest and slowly add the cornflour/cornstarch mixture, still whisking vigorously. Bring to the boil, then remove from the heat. Allow to cool and thicken slightly for 20 minutes. Whisk just to mix, then divide in half.

Ladle one portion of the cream on top of the cake layer in its sealed cake pan. Allow to set for 10 minutes or until a thin film forms on the top, then carefully cover with the second cake layer. Wait for a couple of minutes, then slowly ladle the second portion of cream on top. Allow to cool to room temperature, then refrigerate for at least 6 hours or overnight.

When you are ready to serve, slide a spatula between the cake and the pan to loosen it. Release the pan. The cake should be nice and firm, with a shiny cream all around it. Decorate with chocolate shavings and cut into slices with a sharp knife dipped in hot water.

The cake keeps in the fridge in an airtight container for 5 days.

If you're nuts about nuts, especially hazelnuts, you'll be in heaven after a slice of this cake! Nuts were often used for baking in both my grandmas' kitchens and I favour them too, particularly in the autumn and winter.

Hazelnut heaven cake

Basic Nut Cake (page 19, using hazelnuts and referring to method here)

120 g/¾ cup toasted hazelnuts, roughly chopped, to decorate

FOR THE HAZELNUT CREAM

1.5 litres/6 cups vanilla soy or oat milk

195 g/¾ cup brown rice syrup

2½ teaspoons agar powder or 7 teaspoons agar flakes

160 g/1 cup toasted hazelnuts or 100 g/½ cup hazelnut butter

3 tablespoons vanilla pudding powder or cornflour/cornstarch

28-cm/11-in. or 23-cm/9-in. springform cake pan, baselined with parchment paper and oiled (see method)

Serves 8–15

For the Basic Nut Cake on page 19, decide which size you want to make before you start: a 23-cm/9-in. cake for 8–12 slices or a 28-cm/11-in. cake for 12–15 slices, then follow the corresponding instructions, using hazelnuts. When you've baked the cake and prepared it as described on page 19, put the bottom layer back in the cake pan and set the top layer aside while you make the filling.

For the hazelnut cream, put the milk and syrup in a large saucepan and add the agar. Whisk and bring to the boil over medium heat. As soon as it comes to the boil, lower the heat before it bubbles over and makes a mess! Boil gently for 4–5 minutes if you are using agar powder, or 10–12 minutes if you are using flakes or until the flakes have completely melted.

Meanwhile, if using whole toasted hazelnuts, grind 100 g/⅔ cup of the 160 g/1 cup and finely grind them in a spice mill or food processor. Coarsely chop the rest and set aside.

Mix the vanilla powder or cornflour/cornstarch into 3 tablespoons cold water.

Add the ground nuts or nut butter to the hot cream, whisking vigorously until completely incorporated, then lower the heat to its lowest and slowly add the vanilla powder or cornflour/cornstarch mixture, still whisking vigorously. Bring to the boil, then remove from the heat. Allow to cool and thicken slightly – about 20 minutes. Whisk just to mix, then divide in half.

Ladle one portion of the warm cream on top of the cake layer in its sealed cake pan. Sprinkle the reserved chopped hazelnuts all over the cream. Allow to set for 10 minutes or until a thin film forms on the top, then carefully cover with the second cake layer. Wait for a couple of minutes, then slowly ladle the second portion of cream on top. Allow to cool to room temperature, then refrigerate for at least 6 hours or overnight.

When you are ready to serve, slide a spatula between the cake and the pan to loosen it. Release the pan. The cake should be nice and firm, with a shiny cream all around it. To decorate, scatter the chopped 120 g/¾ cup hazelnuts over the cake and cut into slices with a sharp knife dipped in hot water.

The cake keeps in the fridge in an airtight container for 5 days.

This cake is my husband's firm favourite! If you also like cakes that are more robust and quite filling, this should be your choice. It's a great recipe as it's quite simple and you can use other fruit instead of strawberries; I often use sour cherries, but bananas are great too, especially if the cake is for guests with a serious sweet tooth!

Double cocoa and strawberry cake

Basic Chocolate Cake (page 18, but see method here)

500 g/1 lb. strawberries

FOR THE COCOA BUTTERCREAM

200 g/1 cup Demerara or other good-quality brown sugar (or icing/confectioners' sugar – see method)

150 g/1⅔ cups cocoa powder

½ teaspoon bourbon vanilla powder

450 g/3¼ cups non-hydrogenated margarine, at room temperature

2-3 tablespoons plain soy milk, at room temperature

28-cm/11-in. or 23-cm/9-in. springform cake pan, baselined with parchment paper and oiled (see method)

Serves 8–15

For the Basic Chocolate Cake on page 18, decide which size you want to make before you start: a 23-cm/9-in. cake for 8–12 slices or a 28-cm/11-in. cake for 12–15 slices, then follow the corresponding instructions. When you've baked the cake and prepared it as described on page 18, put the bottom layer on a serving plate and set the top layer aside while you make the filling.

For the cocoa buttercream, very finely grind the brown sugar in a spice mill or food processor; you should get about 2 cups powdered sugar.

Sift together the cocoa powder and powdered brown sugar in a bowl. Stir in the vanilla powder.

In a separate, large bowl, beat the margarine with an electric whisk until soft. Gradually add the sifted ingredients, beating well and adding a little milk when the mixture gets dry. Continue to beat until the buttercream is light and fluffy – this will take a couple of minutes, so be patient!

Hull and slice half of the strawberries. Hull and halve the remaining strawberries (or leave some unhulled if you prefer – these will be used to decorate the top of the cake).

Spread half of the cocoa buttercream over the bottom cake layer with a spatula. Arrange the strawberry slices over the buttercream, then cover with the top cake layer. Spread the remaining buttercream over the top of the cake.

Decorate with the strawberry halves.

Store the cake in the fridge, but bring to room temperature for 30 minutes before serving, as the buttercream firms up when chilled.

I love finding kumquats at farmers' markets; their sweet citrus smell always inspires me to find new ways to use them in recipes. Here I've created a cake in which kumquats and lemons balance the heavier cocoa and buttercream. I love the contrast of dark cake with white frosting and bright orange kumquat circles. If you've never tried these lovely little citrus fruits, you must! They are eaten whole (peel and all) and the peel is ultra sweet while the interior is sharp and juicy. If you can't find them, you can decorate the cake with thin segments of orange instead.

Black and white cake with lemon buttercream

Basic Chocolate Cake (page 18, but see method here)

about 8 kumquats, washed, to decorate

FOR THE LEMON BUTTERCREAM

200 g/1 cup Demerara sugar or other good-quality brown sugar (or icing/confectioners' sugar – see method)

500 g/3½ cups non-hydrogenated margarine, at room temperature

7 tablespoons freshly squeezed lemon juice

2–3 tablespoons finely grated lemon zest

¼ teaspoon bourbon vanilla powder

2 tablespoons plain soy milk, at room temperature

23-cm/9-in. springform cake pan, baselined with parchment paper and oiled

Serves about 12

Make and bake the Basic Chocolate Cake on page 18, then when it has cooled and you have prepared it as described on page 18, put the bottom layer on a serving plate and set the top layer aside while you make the filling.

For the lemon buttercream, very finely grind the brown sugar in a spice mill or food processor; you should get about 2 cups powdered sugar.

In a separate, large bowl, beat the margarine with an electric whisk until soft. Gradually add the powdered brown sugar half a cup at a time, together with a splash of lemon juice. Beat well and keep adding sugar and lemon juice until you have used them all up. Add the lemon zest and the vanilla powder, and a little of the milk, if it is too dry. Mix again until light and fluffy.

Spread one-third of the lemon buttercream over the bottom cake layer with a spatula. Cover with the top cake layer and spread the remaining buttercream over the top and side of the cake, covering it as evenly and neatly as you can.

To decorate, thinly slice the kumquats (peel included) and arrange over the top of the cake.

Store the cake in the fridge, but always bring to room temperature for about 30 minutes before serving, as the buttercream firms up when chilled! Enjoy!

Schwarzwald, or Black-Forest cake is so very popular with my friends and family that I had to come up with a vegan version of it, and when I finally did, I made it into these cupcakes! The chocolate-cherry-whipped-cream combination is a winner, and the high quality of the ingredients used makes them so much tastier than other Schwarzwald desserts!

Black-forest-gâteau cupcakes

130 g/1 cup unbleached plain/
  all-purpose flour

65 g/½ cup plain wholemeal/
  whole-wheat flour

80 g/½ cup semolina/farina

45 g/½ cup cocoa powder

2 teaspoons baking powder

1 teaspoon bicarbonate of/
  baking soda

¼ teaspoon salt

100 g/½ cup sunflower oil

260 g/1 cup brown rice syrup

170 ml/¾ cup plain soy milk

1 teaspoon freshly squeezed
  lemon juice

grated zest of 2 lemons

60 g/½ cup chopped vegan
  dark/bittersweet chocolate

360 g/1½ cups cherries in
  Kirsch

1 teaspoon arrowroot powder

whipped soy cream, to
  decorate

**FOR THE CHOCOLATE
FROSTING**

130 g/1 cup finely chopped
  vegan dark/bittersweet
  chocolate

50 ml/scant ¼ cup non-dairy
  milk

2 tablespoons brown rice syrup

*12-hole muffin pan lined with
  paper cupcake cases*

Makes 12

Preheat the oven to 180°C (350°F) Gas 4.

Mix together the flours, semolina/farina, cocoa powder, baking powder, bicarbonate of/baking soda and salt in a bowl.

In a separate bowl, mix together the oil, syrup, milk, lemon juice and zest. Pour into the bowl of dry ingredients and mix gently with a wooden spoon until just incorporated. Fold in the chocolate.

Divide the cake mixture between the muffin cases.

Bake in the preheated oven for 20–25 minutes. Allow to cool for a few minutes, then remove the cupcakes from the muffin pan and allow to cool completely on a wire rack.

For the chocolate frosting, melt the chocolate in a heatproof bowl set over a saucepan of simmering water. Do not let the base of the bowl touch the water. Meanwhile, heat the milk in a pan until just before boiling. Pour the melted chocolate into the hot milk and whisk until smooth. Add the syrup and mix well. Allow to cool for 45 minutes or until set.

Drain the cherries, saving the Kirsch. Mix the arrowroot into a couple of teaspoons of cold water, then stir into the reserved Kirsch in a pan. Set over medium heat and whisk until it thickens a little – about 2 minutes.

Scoop a little well out of the top of each cooled cupcake with a teaspoon. Carefully pour about 1 teaspoon Kirsch syrup in each well. Place a cherry in there too. Briefly whisk the cooled chocolate frosting, then spread over the cupcakes. Spoon a dollop of whipped soy cream onto each cupcake, top with a couple of cherries and a drizzle of the Kirsch syrup. Serve immediately!

My friend Sanja wanted to surprise her boyfriend with a cake that combined two of his favourite flavours: pineapple and coconut. After serious thinking, testing and retesting, I came up with this, the ultimate summer cake.

Exotic pineapple and coconut cake

Basic Nut Cake (page 19, using desiccated coconut and referring to method here)

FOR THE COCONUT CREAM
500 ml/2¼ cups plain or vanilla soy or oat milk

150 g/generous ½ cup brown rice syrup

1 teaspoon agar powder or 2 teaspoons agar flakes

1 small apple

55 g/3 tablespoons nonhydrogenated margarine

330 g/1½ cups vanilla soy custard

140 g/1¾ cups desiccated coconut, plus extra, toasted, to decorate

3 tablespoons cornflour/cornstarch

FOR THE PINEAPPLE CREAM
1 litre/4⅓ cups vanilla soy or oat milk

100 g/generous ⅓ cup brown rice syrup

1½ teaspoons agar powder or 5 teaspoons agar flakes

300 g/2 cups cubed fresh or canned pineapple

230 ml/1 cup soy cream

grated zest of 1 lemon

2 tablespoons cornflour/cornstarch

28-cm/11-in. or 23-cm/9-in. springform cake pan, base lined with parchment paper and oiled (see method)

Serves 8–15

For the Basic Nut Cake on page 19, decide which size you want to make: a 23-cm/9-in. cake for 8–12 slices or a 28-cm/11-in. cake for 12–15 slices, then follow the corresponding instructions, using desiccated coconut. When you've baked the cake and prepared it as described, put the bottom layer back in the pan and set the top aside while you make the filling.

For the coconut cream, put the milk and 85 g/⅓ cup of the syrup in a large saucepan and add the agar. Whisk and bring to the boil, then lower the heat and simmer for 3 minutes if you are using agar powder, or 8 minutes if using flakes or until the flakes have completely melted.

Peel, core and chop the apple, then put in a food processor with the margarine, remaining syrup and custard. Blend until smooth, then fold in the coconut. Mix the cornflour/cornstarch into 3 tablespoons cold water.

Add the coconut mixture to the hot milk, whisking vigorously until incorporated, then lower the heat to its lowest and slowly add the cornflour/cornstarch mixture, still whisking vigorously. Bring to the boil, then remove from the heat. Pour it on top of the cake layer in its sealed cake pan and spread level with a spatula, then carefully cover with the second cake layer and press gently.

For the pineapple cream, put the milk and syrup in a large pan, add the agar and cook as above. Put the pineapple, cream and lemon zest in a food processor and blend until smooth. Mix the cornflour/cornstarch into 2 tablespoons cold water. Add the pineapple mix to the hot milk, whisking vigorously until incorporated, then lower the heat to its lowest and slowly add the cornflour/cornstarch mix, still whisking vigorously. Bring to the boil, then remove from the heat. Ladle two-thirds of the cream on top of the second cake in the pan. Chill the remaining cream for later. Let the cake to cool to room temperature, then chill for at least 6 hours or overnight.

When ready to serve, slide a spatula between the cake and the pan to loosen and release the pan. The cake should be firm, with a shiny cream all around it. Briefly whisk the chilled pineapple cream until smooth, then spread around the side of the cake. Scatter toasted desiccated coconut over the top and cut into slices with a sharp knife dipped in hot water. The cake keeps in the fridge in an airtight container for 5 days.

According to a survey from 2011, carrot cake was voted as the favourite cake in the UK! I'm offering you a recipe that contains the expected ingredients (carrots, walnuts, raisins) but it is sweetened with maple syrup, it's low in fat and the frosting is very light.

Rich carrot cake

200 g/1½ cups unbleached plain/all-purpose flour

65 g/½ cup plain wholemeal/whole-wheat flour

1 teaspoon baking powder

1 teaspoon bicarbonate of/baking soda

¼ teaspoon salt

1 teaspoon ground cinnamon

40 g/1 cup desiccated coconut

½ teaspoon bourbon vanilla powder

100 g/½ cup coconut oil

170 g/⅔ cup pure maple syrup

freshly squeezed juice and grated zest of 1 orange, plus extra to decorate

½ teaspoon apple cider vinegar

1 teaspoon rum

330 g/3 cups grated carrots

60 g/½ cup raisins

80 g/½ cup chopped walnuts

FOR THE FROSTING

220 ml/1 cup oat milk

2 tablespoons oat or soy cream

3 tablespoons pure maple syrup

3 scant tablespoons cornflour/cornstarch

½ teaspoon bourbon vanilla powder

6 drops of pure orange extract or 1 tablespoon finely grated orange zest

23-cm/9-in. springform cake pan, baselined with parchment paper and oiled

Serves about 8

Preheat the oven to 180°C (350°F) Gas 4.

Sift together the flours, baking powder, bicarbonate of/baking soda, salt and cinnamon in a bowl, add the desiccated coconut and vanilla powder and mix well.

If the coconut oil has solidified, put the jar in a bowl of hot water until the oil has softened.

In a separate bowl, mix together the syrup, coconut oil, orange juice and zest, vinegar and rum.

Combine both bowls and mix until smooth. Add the carrots, raisins and walnuts and fold in with a spatula. The mixture will be thicker than a normal cake mixture. Spoon the cake mixture into the prepared cake pan and spread level with a spatula. Bake in the preheated oven for 30 minutes. Allow to cool completely in the pan.

For the frosting, put all the ingredients in a small saucepan and whisk well for the cornflour/cornstarch to dissolve. Set over medium heat and whisk vigorously for a couple of minutes. As the milk starts to warm up, the cornflour/cornstarch will start to thicken it. As soon as the frosting is thick enough to spread, remove it from heat.

Remove the cake from the pan and spread the hot frosting over the top with a spatula. Allow to cool completely.

Decorate the cake with orange zest and drizzle a little maple syrup on each slice to make it sweeter, if you like.

CHAPTER 3

Slices and bars

For lunchboxes, picnics and after-school treats – these slices and bars are usually nutritious, often portable and always delicious! Some of the recipes in this chapter are so simple that children can help you make them. They will love to get their hands messy and then to tuck into the fruits of their labours afterwards.

Carob is native to the Mediterranean region but can now be found in stores everywhere – as powder, syrup, drops, spread, etc. It is sometimes used as a cocoa substitute as it tastes similar but contains no caffeine. These slices are sweet and full of carob flavour, and most people who have never tasted carob before say that it was love at first bite!

Yummy carob slices

675 ml/3 cups plain soy milk

100 g/3½ oz. carob 'chocolate', finely chopped

2 teaspoons apple cider vinegar

195 g/¾ cup brown rice syrup

150 g/¾ cup sunflower oil

1 tablespoon ground flaxseeds

415 g/3 cups plus 2 tablespoons unbleached plain/all-purpose flour

65 g/½ cup plain wholemeal/whole-wheat flour

75 g/¾ cup carob powder, for dusting

1½ teaspoons bicarbonate of/baking soda

1½ teaspoons baking powder

½ teaspoon salt

¼ teaspoon bourbon vanilla powder

FOR THE CAROB GLAZE

3 tablespoons cornflour/cornstarch

550 ml/2 cups non-dairy milk

170 g/⅔ cup carob syrup or pure maple syrup

180 g/1¾ cups carob powder

1 teaspoon agar powder or 2 teaspoons agar flakes

40 x 28-cm/16 x 11-in. baking pan, lined with parchment paper

Makes about 20

Preheat the oven to 180°C (350°F) Gas 4.

Heat 250 ml/1 cup of the milk in a large saucepan until hot but not boiling, then remove from the heat, add the carob 'chocolate' and allow to melt.

Mix together the remaining milk and the vinegar in a bowl and set aside for 2–3 minutes.

Stir the melted carob until smooth, then add the vinegar mixture. Add the syrup, oil and flaxseeds and whisk until combined.

Sift together the flours, carob powder, bicarbonate of/baking soda, baking powder, salt and vanilla powder in a mixing bowl.

Slowly pour the wet ingredients into the sifted dry ingredients, mixing with a wooden spoon. Do not overmix but try to get a smooth mixture without too many lumps.

Spoon the cake mixture into the prepared baking pan and spread level with a spatula. Bake in the preheated oven for 30 minutes or until a skewer inserted in the middle comes out clean. Allow to cool completely in the pan.

For the carob glaze, mix the cornflour/cornstarch into 4 tablespoons cold water.

Put the milk, syrup, carob powder and agar in a saucepan and mix well. Bring to the boil, then lower the heat and simmer for a couple of minutes. Slowly add the cornflour/cornstarch mixture, whisking vigorously. Bring to the boil, then remove from the heat.

Pour the hot carob glaze over the cooled cake in the pan. Spread it with a spatula and allow to cool at room temperature for 1–2 hours.

Dust with carob powder and cut into slices to serve.

I remember eating a dessert similar to this one at my neighbour's house a couple of times and I really liked the texture, but the taste of butter in the glaze was too strong and the cake was too sweet. So I made a vegan version of it, leaving semolina/farina as the main ingredient but adapting it to my taste. You can also use half semolina/farina and half unbleached flour, but the grainy texture is what makes these squares so interesting. Also, the coconut oil in the glaze definitely works much better than butter!

Sticky mocha squares

30 g/⅓ cup cocoa powder

2 teaspoons bicarbonate of/ baking soda

360 g/2 cups semolina/farina

¼ teaspoon salt

230 ml/1 cup plain soy yogurt

230 ml/1 cup plain soy milk (vanilla-flavoured or plain)

½ teaspoon apple cider vinegar

100 g/½ cup sunflower oil

195 g/¾ cup pure maple syrup

1 teaspoon coffee extract

FOR THE GLAZE

100 g/½ cup coconut oil

170 ml/¾ cup non-dairy milk

100 g/3½ oz. vegan dark/ bittersweet chocolate, finely chopped

¼ teaspoon bourbon vanilla powder

4 tablespoons brown rice or pure maple syrup

1 teaspoon coffee extract

23 x 30-cm/9 x 12-in. baking pan, oiled

Makes about 20

Preheat the oven to 180°C (350°F) Gas 4.

Sift together the cocoa powder and bicarbonate of/baking soda in a mixing bowl, then mix in the semolina/farina and salt.

In a separate bowl, whisk together the yogurt, milk, vinegar, oil, syrup and coffee extract. Pour into the bowl of dry ingredients and mix with a wooden spoon until combined.

Spoon the cake mixture into the prepared baking pan and spread level with a spatula. Bake in the preheated oven for 25 minutes.

Meanwhile, for the glaze, if the coconut oil has solidified, put the jar in a bowl of hot water until the oil has softened.

Heat the milk in a saucepan until hot but not boiling, then remove from the heat, add the chocolate and allow to melt. Stir until smooth.

Add the coconut oil, vanilla powder, syrup and coffee extract to the pan and whisk to get a smooth glaze. Keep warm until the cake has finished baking.

Pour the glaze over the hot cake in the pan and allow to cool completely. Most of the glaze will be absorbed by the cake and this is what makes it so moist.

Serve at room temperature on the day of baking if possible (or the next day), cut into slices.

These slices are a coconut-lover's heaven; they are creamy and rich, and the fluffy vanilla-flavoured frosting topped with loads of coconut and combined with a slightly crunchy base makes you wish for another portion, and another, and another...

Raffaello slices

130 g/1 cup unbleached plain/
all-purpose flour

2 tablespoons cornflour/
cornstarch

1 teaspoon baking powder

a pinch of salt

a pinch of ground turmeric

55 g/⅔ cup desiccated coconut

100 g/½ cup sunflower oil

180 g/⅔ cup brown rice syrup

2 tablespoons plain soy milk

½ teaspoon vanilla extract

1 teaspoon lemon juice or
apple cider vinegar

FOR THE FROSTING

5 tablespoons cornflour/
cornstarch

365 ml/1⅔ cups vanilla-
flavoured soy milk

100 g/½ cup raw/unrefined
brown sugar, plus 2
tablespoons

¼ teaspoon vanilla bourbon
powder

a pinch of ground turmeric

100 g/¾ cup margarine,
at room temperature

55 g/⅔ cup desiccated coconut,
lightly toasted

*24 x 17-cm/9½ x 7-in. baking
pan, oiled*

Makes about 24

Preheat the oven to 160°C (325°F) Gas 3.

Sift together the flour, cornflour/cornstarch and baking powder in a mixing bowl, then mix in the salt, turmeric and coconut.

In a separate bowl, mix the oil, syrup, milk, vanilla extract and lemon juice or vinegar. Pour into the bowl of dry ingredients and mix gently with a spatula until combined.

Spoon the mixture evenly into the prepared baking pan, pressing it down lightly. This mixture is thicker than you might expect – it slightly resembles moist cookie dough. Put it in the preheated oven and check it after 10 minutes and every couple of minutes thereafter. Remove it from the oven as soon as you see a slight change in colour. If you wait until it gets golden brown, you might end up with a tasty but quite hard base that will be difficult to eat with a fork. When it is ready, remove it from the oven, allow it to cool for a couple of minutes, then cover it with clingfilm/plastic wrap to keep it soft. Allow to cool completely.

For the frosting, mix the cornflour/cornstarch into 120 ml/½ cup of the milk, then stir in the 2 tablespoons brown sugar, the vanilla powder and turmeric.

Heat the remaining milk in a saucepan until boiling, then remove from the heat and slowly add the cornflour/cornstarch mixture, whisking vigorously. Put back over low heat and whisk for a minute until the sticky cream starts bubbling. Remove from the heat, allow to cool completely and whisk until smooth again.

Very finely grind the remaining sugar in a spice mill or food processor. In a bowl, beat the margarine with an electric whisk until soft. Gradually add the powdered sugar and beat until light and fluffy. Now add the vanilla cream, gently mixing with a spatula to get an even, smooth frosting.

Spread the frosting evenly over the cooled base. Sprinkle the coconut over it to cover completely. Wrap in foil and refrigerate for a couple of hours before cutting into slices, to serve.

I've been eating this dessert since I can remember and baking it since primary school. You can use nearly any seasonal produce and it will turn out tasty. I prefer using slightly sour fruit like sour cherries, cherry plums or apricots but it also works well with ripe peaches, apples and raspberries, for example. Frozen or canned fruit can also be used if you don't have any fresh fruit to hand.

Fruit-topped bars

260 g/2 cups unbleached spelt flour

65 g/½ cup plain wholemeal/ whole-wheat flour

1 teaspoon bicarbonate of/ baking soda

1½ teaspoons baking powder

¼ teaspoon salt

¼ teaspoon bourbon vanilla powder

¼ teaspoon ground cinnamon

a few pinches of ground turmeric

80 g/½ cup hazelnuts or almonds, chopped

360 ml/1½ cups plain soy yogurt

170 g/⅔ cup pure maple syrup

100 g/½ cup coconut, safflower or other good-quality oil

freshly squeezed juice and grated zest of 1 lemon

1 teaspoon apple cider vinegar

350 g/2 cups pitted sour cherries or cherry plums

23 x 30-cm/9 x 12-in. baking pan, lined with parchment paper

Makes about 20

Preheat the oven to 180°C (350°F) Gas 4.

Sift together the flours, bicarbonate of/baking soda, baking powder, salt, vanilla powder, cinnamon and turmeric. Add the nuts and mix together.

In a separate bowl, mix the yogurt, syrup, oil, lemon juice and zest and vinegar. Pour into the bowl of dry ingredients and mix gently with a wooden spoon. Do not overmix.

Spoon the mixture into the prepared baking pan and spread level with a spatula. Scatter the cherries or plums over the surface of the cake mixture, making sure there is some space between the fruit – you don't want to overload the cake with fruit otherwise it will turn out soggy.

Bake the cake in the preheated oven for about 35 minutes, or until golden brown. Remove from the oven and allow to cool in the pan.

Slice into squares and drizzle maple syrup over the top to serve.

At first, the idea of using cooked beans in a brownie mixture might not sound too promising or appealing. However, blended beans give a wonderful texture to the brownies and it's a great way to introduce plant protein to kids or people who wouldn't want to eat a bean stew for lunch. Cashews can be replaced by other nuts, but I suggest you try this wonderful combination; you won't be sorry!

Bean and cashew brownies

300 g/2 cups canned unsalted haricot/navy beans (see method for an alternative)

200 g/1½ cups finely chopped vegan dark/bittersweet chocolate (70% cocoa)

65 g/⅓ cup sunflower oil

130 g/½ cup brown rice or pure maple syrup

freshly squeezed juice and grated zest of 1 lemon

80 g/½ cup whole or 80 g/ 1 cup finely ground cashews

85 g/⅔ cup unbleached plain/ all-purpose flour

40 g/⅓ cup plain wholemeal/ whole-wheat flour

1 tablespoon baking powder

¼ teaspoon salt

¼ teaspoon ground cinnamon

2 tablespoons apricot jam, for serving

23 x 30-cm/9 x 12-in. baking pan, oiled

Makes about 20

If you want to cook the haricot/navy beans from scratch, soak 140 g/ ¾ cup dried beans in a lot of water overnight. Drain, cover with three times the volume of water and cook for 1 hour (or 40 minutes in a pressure cooker). Drain well.

Preheat the oven to 180°C (350°F) Gas 4.

Melt the chocolate in a heatproof bowl set over a saucepan of simmering water. Do not let the base of the bowl touch the water.

Put the melted chocolate, cooked beans, oil, syrup, lemon juice and zest in a food processor and blend until smooth.

If using whole cashews, finely grind them in a food processor or spice mill. Mix the flours, ground cashews, baking powder, salt and ground cinnamon in a mixing bowl. Add the bean mixture and fold in with a spatula until you get a smooth, thick consistency (much thicker than usual cake mixtures).

Spoon the cake mixture into the prepared baking pan and spread level with a spatula; if it sticks too much, wet it with warm water and try again. Bake in the preheated oven for 15–20 minutes. Do not overbake – they are supposed to be a little gooey! Allow to cool completely in the baking pan.

Cut into squares to serve. I like to serve them with a little homemade apricot jam which contrasts beautifully with the rich, heavy chocolate taste of these brownies.

These yummy treats do look funny – furry and white from all the coconut they have been rolled in! This is a recipe that I tried to 'veganize' while still in high-school. It became quite popular and I know for a fact that it was the first cake a couple of my school friends attempted to make. So I assure you, you can make them too!

Lamingtons

80 g/½ cup almonds or 80 g/ 1 cup ground almonds

260 g/2 cups unbleached plain/ all-purpose flour

45 g/⅓ cup oat flour

1 tablespoon cornflour/ cornstarch

1 teaspoon baking powder

1 teaspoon bicarbonate of/ baking soda

¼ teaspoon salt

a pinch of saffron threads

100 g/½ cup safflower or sunflower oil

170 g/⅔ cup brown rice syrup

350 ml/1½ cups plain soy milk

1 teaspoon vanilla extract

160 g/2 cups desiccated coconut

FOR THE GLAZE

300 ml/1⅓ cups non-dairy milk

50 g/⅓ cup margarine

70 g/½ cup finely chopped vegan dark/bittersweet chocolate

130 g/⅔ cup Demerara sugar

23 x 30-cm/9 x 12-in. baking pan, oiled

Makes 12

Preheat the oven to 180°C (350°F) Gas 4. Dust the baking pan with a little flour to coat the base and shake off any excess.

If using whole almonds, lightly roast them for a couple of minutes in the preheated oven, then finely grind them in a food processor or spice mill.

Sift the ground almonds, both flours, cornflour/cornstarch, baking powder, bicarbonate of/baking soda and salt in a mixing bowl and stir in the saffron threads.

In a separate bowl, mix the oil, syrup, milk and vanilla extract. Pour into the bowl of dry ingredients and mix gently with a wooden spoon. Do not overmix.

Pour the mixture into the prepared baking pan and spread level with a spatula. Bake in the preheated oven for 20 minutes. Allow to cool completely in the pan, then cut into 12 squares.

Put the coconut on a big plate.

When the cake has cooled, for the glaze, put all ingredients in a saucepan over low heat and whisk occasionally until the margarine and chocolate have melted and the sugar has dissolved. Stir until smooth. Pour the hot glaze into a wide, shallow container or a small baking pan. Dip each cooled cake square into it, waiting for it to soak up some of the glaze all over before taking it out with a fork. Don't be impatient – if you just dip the squares in too quickly, you'll have a lot of glaze left and the lamingtons won't be moist.

Use a fork to roll each square in the coconut. Try to do it neatly as the glaze can stick to the coconut and your squares won't look nice and white.

Allow to cool before serving. If you do happen to have some glaze left, drizzle it over each square before serving. Enjoy!

Home-baked bars are so easy to make and you'll be grateful to find them in your cupboard whenever you crave sweets or need a takeaway breakfast or healthy snack. Kids love to get these in their lunchboxes and grandmas love to dip them into warm soy milk after their afternoon nap (well, at least lactose-intolerant grandmas like mine!). Use any syrup you have available; agave, rice, maple, apple, date – they all work well in this recipe.

Oat bars filled with jam

300 g/3 cups rolled oats

130 g/1 cup unbleached spelt flour

½ teaspoon bourbon vanilla powder

½ teaspoon ground cinnamon

1 teaspoon baking powder

½ teaspoon salt

170 g/⅔ cup brown rice syrup (see Introduction above)

130 g/½ cup coconut or sunflower oil

90 g/4 tablespoons naturally sweetened fruit jam

23 x 30-cm/9 x 12-inch baking pan, greased

Makes 12

Preheat the oven to 180°C (350°F) Gas 4.

Mix the oats, flour, vanilla powder, cinnamon, baking powder and salt in a mixing bowl, then add the syrup and oil and mix thoroughly with a wooden spoon.

Spoon half the dough into the prepared baking pan and press down evenly into the pan. Spread the fruit preserve over the dough with a wet spatula, then spoon over the remaining dough, smoothing the top with a spatula.

Bake in the preheated oven for 20 minutes. Remove from the baking pan and allow to cool on a wire rack.

Cut into squares to serve. Refrigerated, they'll keep for 2 weeks in an airtight container but it's more likely they'll be gone in 2 days!

Variation: You could also try filling these with hazelnut or carob spread.

CHAPTER 4

Cookies and biscuits

For the cookie jar, a surprise visit from a friend, a late-night snack or to accompany a cup of coffee – it needn't take long to whip up a batch of bite-size cookies and biscuits to munch on throughout the week. Whether you keep them simple and wholesome, or a little more refined with a drizzle of chocolate, it's up to you!

As the mums of all my best friends know I love baking, I occasionally get emails from them with interesting recipes for their favourite desserts. Although they always contain milk, butter and lots of sugar, they always inspire me and I often end up making a vegan version that everybody likes even more than the original! The same story goes for these apricot and chocolate bites; the Krpan family were kind enough to reveal a similar recipe that has since become a part of my sweet repertoire too.

Apricot and chocolate bites

100 g/⅔ cup unsulfured dried apricots, chopped

freshly squeezed juice and grated zest of 1 big orange

¼ teaspoon ground ginger

80 g/1 cup desiccated coconut

150 g/1 cup plus 2 tablespoons unbleached plain/all-purpose flour

¼ teaspoon salt

100 g/½ cup coconut oil

70 g/¼ cup brown rice or other syrup

50 g/⅓ cup finely chopped vegan dark/bittersweet chocolate

¼ teaspoon sunflower oil

baking sheets, lined with parchment paper

Makes 32–35

Preheat the oven to 160°C (325°F) Gas 3.

Put the apricots, orange juice and zest and ginger in a small saucepan over medium heat. Heat until hot but not boiling. Remove from the heat and transfer to a food processor. Blend to a paste but don't worry if a few chunks remain.

Put the coconut in a heavy frying pan/skillet and toast over medium–low heat, stirring occasionally, until pale golden – about 8 minutes. Do not burn! Remove from the pan and allow to cool slightly.

Mix the flour and salt in a bowl and add the toasted coconut.

If the coconut oil has solidified, put the jar in a bowl of hot water until the oil has softened. Add it to the apricot paste with the syrup and mix well. Now add this to the dry ingredients in the bowl and mix with a wooden spoon until well incorporated.

Use a small spoon to scoop portions of dough onto the prepared baking sheets. Shape into balls, then flatten slightly with the back of the spoon. You should get about 32–35 cookies. Bake the cookies in batches in the preheated oven for 10–12 minutes, just until lightly golden. If you overbake them, they will become tough. Allow to cool for a couple of minutes, then transfer to a wire rack to cool completely.

Melt the chocolate in a heatproof bowl set over a saucepan of simmering water. Do not let the base of the bowl touch the water. Add the oil and stir until smooth, then allow to cool slightly.

Dip each cookie halfway into the melted chocolate. Allow to cool and set completely before serving. Store in an airtight container for up to 2 weeks.

Almost all cookie recipes (at least the ones that I make) are very simple; you can have a freshly baked batch in less than 30 minutes, and these are no exception. The mix of spices makes them more of a winter choice, but feel free to use other spices, or omit them – it won't change their crunchiness or yumminess at all!

Spicy oat cookies with cashews

100 g/1 cup rolled oats

160 g/1 cup cashews

130 g/1 cup unbleached plain/ all-purpose flour

¼ teaspoon baking powder

½ teaspoon ground cinnamon

¼ teaspoon ground nutmeg

¼ teaspoon ground ginger

a pinch of chilli powder (optional)

¼ teaspoon salt

130 g/½ cup pure maple syrup

100 g/½ cup coconut or sunflower oil

1 tablespoon ground flaxseeds

baking sheets, lined with parchment paper

Makes about 30

Preheat the oven to 180°C (350°F) Gas 4.

Coarsely grind the oats in a food processor or spice mill. Finely grind the cashews in the same way.

Sift the flour, baking powder, cinnamon, nutmeg, ginger, chilli powder and salt in a bowl, then stir in the ground oats and cashews. Mix well.

Put the syrup, oil and flaxseeds in a separate bowl and whisk vigorously. Pour into the bowl of dry ingredients and mix with a wooden spoon.

Pull off walnut-sized pieces of dough and roll into balls. Arrange on the baking sheets about 3 cm/1¼ inches apart. Gently flatten each ball with the help of an oiled spatula or fish slice.

Bake the cookies in batches in the preheated oven for 10–12 minutes, and take them out as soon as the bottoms turn slightly golden. Don't worry if they seem soft – they will harden as they cool down.

Remove from the oven, transfer to a wire rack and allow to cool. Store in an airtight container for up to 2 weeks.

One day, as I was getting ready to bake a batch of cookies and was reaching for ingredients in my cupboard, a jar of couscous wouldn't get out of my way... It was obvious I had to use couscous in the cookie dough, so I did. And look what I created! This is a great cookie with a crunchy texture, a maple aroma and a slightly soft centre filled with jam. I cannot think of a better way to use up some of the plum jam that I make in the summer to enjoy throughout the year.

Couscous and jam crunchies

120 g/¾ cup couscous

160 g/1¾ cups ground almonds

130 g/1 cup unbleached plain/all-purpose flour

1 tablespoon ground flaxseeds

¼ teaspoon bourbon vanilla powder

¼ teaspoon salt

130 g/½ cup pure maple syrup

100 g/½ cup sunflower oil

½ teaspoon almond extract

24 teaspoons/200 g/⅔ cup plum or other thick, naturally sweetened jam

baking sheets, lined with parchment paper

Makes about 24

Preheat the oven to 180°C (350°F) Gas 4.

Put the couscous, almonds, flour, flaxseeds, vanilla powder and salt in a mixing bowl and mix.

Put the syrup, oil and almond extract in a separate bowl and whisk vigorously. Pour into the bowl of dry ingredients and mix with a wooden spoon.

Pull off walnut-sized pieces of dough and roll into balls. Flatten them between your palms until 1 cm/½ inch thick. Arrange them on the baking sheets spaced just slightly apart – they won't spread during baking.

Now use the bottom of a teaspoon, or even better, a teaspoon-sized measuring spoon to gently press a hole in the middle of each cookie. Make circle motions to widen the hole, but don't press too hard otherwise you might break through the bottom of the cookie. Fill each hole with a full teaspoon of jam. Bake in the preheated oven for 15–16 minutes. Don't worry if they seem soft – they will harden as they cool down.

Remove from the oven and allow to cool on the baking sheets. Store in an airtight container for up to 2 weeks.

There are people who love coconut, and there are those who don't. I personally cannot understand what there is not to like! Coconut is just so wonderful in all its forms and I get jealous of people living in countries where you can buy young coconuts, drink the water, use up the flesh in smoothies and enjoy its wonderful taste and texture. But then I bake these cookies and I'm happy that desiccated coconut is a product available in many stores, wherever I am!

My favourite coconut cookies

130 g/1 cup unbleached spelt or unbleached plain/all-purpose flour

¼ teaspoon bicarbonate of/baking soda

¼ teaspoon salt

¼ teaspoon vanilla bourbon powder

160 g/2 cups desiccated coconut

75 g/⅓ cup coconut or soy milk

135 g/⅔ cup Demerara sugar

65 g/⅓ cup coconut or sunflower oil

1 tablespoon ground flaxseeds (optional)

50 g/⅓ cup finely chopped vegan dark/bittersweet chocolate

baking sheet, lined with parchment paper

Makes about 20

Preheat the oven to 180°C (350°F) Gas 4.

Sift together the flour, bicarbonate of/baking soda, salt and vanilla powder in a bowl, then stir in the desiccated coconut.

Put the milk, sugar, oil and flaxseeds, if using, in a separate bowl and whisk vigorously until well combined. Pour into the bowl of dry ingredients and mix with a spatula until you get dough that is firm but a little sticky – it shouldn't be dry or crumbly.

Wet your hands and pull off a tablespoon of the dough. You can either roll it into a ball and flatten it between your palms to get a flat, round cookie, or, what I do is roll the tablespoon of dough into a sausage and then flatten it into a flat oval. That makes them easier to dip into tea or hot cocoa. Also, ovals are convenient if you like writing chocolate messages on cookies, and I do that often!

Continue with the rest of the dough, arranging each cookie 2 cm/¾ inch apart on the prepared baking sheet. Bake in the preheated oven for 8–10 minutes, no longer! Take them out as soon as the bottoms turn slightly golden. Don't worry if they seem pale and a little soft – they will harden as they cool down.

Remove the cookies from the oven, transfer to a wire rack and allow to cool completely.

Melt the chocolate in a heatproof bowl set over a saucepan of simmering water. Do not let the base of the bowl touch the water. Drizzle the melted chocolate over the cooled cookies and allow to set. Store in an airtight container for up to 2 weeks.

Japanese persimmon or kaki is a sweet fruit with a soft texture. It is a species native to China but is now widely spread throughout the Mediterranean too. Beautiful persimmon trees laden with fruits can often be seen in gardens in Istria. I always allow the fruits to ripen and soften after the harvest – this brings out their best flavour.

Drop cookies with persimmon and cranberries

70 g/½ cup coconut oil or non-hydrogenated margarine, at room temperature

170 g/⅔ cup brown rice syrup

250 ml/1 cup persimmon pulp (from 1–2 persimmons), pushed through a sieve/strainer

60 g/½ cup chopped walnuts

60 g/½ cup dried cranberries

200 g/1½ cups unbleached plain/all-purpose flour

60 g/½ cup unbleached spelt or plain wholemeal/whole-wheat flour

2 teaspoons baking powder

½ teaspoon ground cinnamon

¼ teaspoon salt

plain soy milk, as needed

baking sheets, lined with parchment paper

Makes about 26

Preheat the oven to 180°C (350°F) Gas 4.

In a large mixing bowl, beat together the coconut oil or margarine, the syrup and persimmon pulp. Add the walnuts and cranberries and stir through. Sift the flours, baking powder, cinnamon and salt into the bowl and stir in with a wooden spoon. If the dough seems too dry, add a splash of milk but not too much – the dough should be thick enough not to slide off the spoon.

Drop generous tablespoons of the dough onto the prepared baking sheets, about 1 cm/½ inch apart. Bake the cookies in the preheated oven for 15 minutes.

Remove the cookies from the oven and allow to cool on the baking sheets. Store in an airtight container for up to 2 weeks.

My dad adores this treat and he asked me to include it in this cookbook so other people can enjoy it too. Originally, the recipe called for a lot of sugar and many eggs, but the vegan version is so much healthier and tastes even better! Just make sure that the temperature of the ingredients for the dough is right (everything ice-cold!) otherwise the base could turn out crumbly or oily.

Dad's hazelnut triangles

½ quantity Sweet Pie Dough (page 20)

FOR THE HAZELNUT TOPPING

50 g/⅓ cup non-hydrogenated margarine

240 g/1½ cups chopped hazelnuts

50 g/½ cup ground hazelnuts

6 tablespoons non-dairy milk

100 g/½ cup Demerara sugar

¼ teaspoon bourbon vanilla powder

2 tablespoons arrowroot powder or cornflour/cornstarch

1 teaspoon rum

a pinch of salt

23 x 30-cm/9 x 12-in. baking pan

Makes 24

Make and refrigerate the Sweet Pie Dough as described on page 20. Allow the dough to rest at room temperature for 5–10 minutes before rolling it out.

Preheat the oven to 180°C (350°F) Gas 4.

For the hazelnut topping, melt the margarine in a large saucepan over low heat, then remove from the heat and add the chopped and ground hazelnuts, milk, sugar, vanilla powder, arrowroot, rum and salt. Whisk together vigorously.

Place the dough on a sheet of lightly floured parchment paper, dust with a little flour and roll it out to fit the base of the baking pan – about 23 x 30 cm/9 x 12 inches. Brush off any excess flour and transfer the dough, together with the parchment paper, into the pan. Prick it all over with a fork. Bake in the preheated oven for 8 minutes. Leave the oven on.

Remove the pan from the oven and spread the hazelnut topping evenly over the baked base with a spatula.

Put back in the oven and bake for 20–22 minutes, or until starting to turn golden. Don't worry if the topping feels a little soft – it has to cool completely before you can cut it. The best idea is to refrigerate it for a couple of hours.

To serve, cut the cold bake into 24 triangles with a sharp knife. If you try to cut it when it's still warm, the topping will crumble and you'll end up having to eat it with a spoon, so be patient! Serve it with a cup of tea or non-dairy latte. Store in an airtight container for up to 2 weeks.

Vegan biscotti? Yes, it's possible to make them in spite of the fact that the main ingredient holding everything together in conventional biscotti recipes is egg white. Follow my instructions precisely and don't fear, these are even better than the same old regular biscotti! You can use any nuts and spices instead of pistachios and fennel seeds, or try adding a small amount of dried fruit to the mix.

Pistachio and fennel biscotti

200 g/1½ cups unbleached plain/all-purpose flour

½ teaspoon baking powder

½ teaspoon bicarbonate of/ baking soda

¼ teaspoon salt (omit if using salted pistachios)

2 tablespoons arrowroot powder or cornflour/ cornstarch

⅛ teaspoon bourbon vanilla powder

a pinch of ground turmeric

½–1 tablespoon fennel seeds

260 g/2 cups shelled pistachios (raw, unsalted, if available)

80 ml/⅓ cup plain soy milk

65 g/⅓ cup sunflower oil

100 g/½ cup Demerara sugar

freshly squeezed juice and grated zest of 1 lemon

baking sheet, lined with parchment paper

Makes about 20

Preheat the oven to 180°C (350°F) Gas 4.

Sift together the flour, baking powder, bicarbonate of/baking soda, salt, arrowroot, vanilla powder and turmeric in a large bowl. Stir in the fennel seeds and pistachios.

In a separate bowl, whisk together the milk, oil, sugar and lemon juice and zest. Pour into the dry ingredients and stir well with a wooden spoon to form a soft dough that sticks lightly to your fingers. Turn the dough out onto the prepared baking sheet, and, with the help of a silicone spatula, form 2 logs about 27 x 6 cm/10½ x 2½ inches, neatening the edges and ends. Bake in the preheated oven for 20 minutes, or until lightly golden. Allow to cool completely on the baking sheet. Don't skip this step otherwise the biscotti slices will crumble.

Preheat the oven to 150°C (300°F) Gas 2.

Place the biscotti logs on a chopping/cutting board and use a sharp bread knife to cut them, at an angle, into 1-cm/½-inch thick slices. Lay them down carefully on the lined baking sheet. Rebake for about 10–20 minutes, turning the slices over halfway through baking, depending on how crisp you want them. Allow to cool completely on the baking sheet.

Store in a big, long cookie jar hidden at the back of the most remote kitchen cupboard otherwise they'll be gone in a minute! They will keep for up to 2 weeks. Serve with a cup of non-dairy latte or fennel tea!

Even though I don't drink coffee, coffee-flavoured treats immediately go onto my favourite foods list. You can use cocoa powder instead of ground cocoa beans here, but I prefer grinding the beans in a coffee grinder myself – their texture very much resembles freshly ground coffee beans, which is so appropriate for this recipe. The icing gives an additional sweet coffee kick for your taste buds!

Coffee toffee cookies

30 g/⅓ cup raw cocoa beans (or nibs) or 30 g/⅓ cup cocoa powder
100 g/½ cup coconut oil
100 g/½ cup Demerara sugar
60 ml/¼ cup plain soy milk
2 teaspoons coffee extract
¼ teaspoon apple cider vinegar
200 g/1½ cups unbleached spelt flour
½ teaspoon baking powder
1 tablespoon ground flaxseeds
¼ teaspoon bourbon vanilla powder
2 tablespoons ground almonds
¼ teaspoon salt
¼ teaspoon ground cinnamon
chopped nuts, for sprinkling

FOR THE ICING
65 g/⅓ cup Demerara sugar
1 tablespoon cornflour/cornstarch
2 tablespoons plain soy milk
1 teaspoon coffee extract

baking sheets, lined with parchment paper

Makes 25

Preheat the oven to 180°C (350°F) Gas 4.

If using cocoa beans, grind them in a coffee or spice grinder to a fine powder.

If the coconut oil has solidified, put the jar in a bowl of hot water until the oil has softened. Whisk together the oil, sugar, milk, coffee extract and vinegar.

In a separate bowl, sift together the flour and baking powder, then stir in the flaxseeds, vanilla powder, ground almonds, salt and cinnamon. Tip into the bowl of wet ingredients and mix into a smooth dough with a spatula.

Divide the dough into 25 and roll into balls. Arrange them on the prepared baking sheets about 2 cm/¾ inch apart. Gently flatten each ball with the back of a spoon, trying to avoid making cracks. Bake in the preheated oven for 9–10 minutes. Do not overbake them – they should still be a little soft. Allow to cool completely on the baking sheets.

For the icing, it's better to finely grind the sugar in a coffee or spice grinder, but you can also try without grinding it. Mix the cornflour/cornstarch into the milk in a heatproof bowl. Add the coffee extract and sugar and mix. Set over a saucepan of simmering water (do not let the base of the bowl touch the water) and whisk well for a couple of minutes to allow the starch to thicken slightly over the steam. Remove from the heat, then allow to cool for 10 minutes.

Spoon some icing over each cold cookie and sprinkle chopped nuts over the top. Allow to set for at least 1 hour after which the icing shouldn't be sticky, but smooth and firm to the touch.

Store in an airtight container at room temperature, or, in the summer months, in the fridge. They will keep for up to 2 weeks.

CHAPTER 5

Pies, tarts and strudels

For an alternative to a birthday cake, a wintry, warming dessert, a celebration of summer fruit or a slice of comfort after a long day – these recipes come in all shapes, sizes and characters to suit all sorts of needs. Going vegan needn't mean the end of pastry and these pies, tarts and strudels show how much there is to enjoy.

Apple pie must be one of the most baked desserts in my family's kitchen! Pies in general are very popular, but this combination of crumbly crust and the lovely smell and taste of apples combined with cinnamon and raisins is an irresistible and irreplaceable year-round treat! I often bake pies in rectangular baking pans and serve them dusted with a little icing/confectioners' sugar and cinnamon, but you could serve yours with vegan custard if you prefer.

European-style apple pie

Sweet Pie Dough (page 20)

FOR THE FILLING
1.5 kg/3½ lb. apples, peeled
60 g/½ cup raisins
65 g/¼ cup brown rice syrup
½ teaspoon ground cinnamon

40 x 28-cm/16 x 11-in. baking
   pan (for a thinner crust) or
   23 x 30 cm/9 x 12-in. baking
   pan (for a thicker crust)

Serves about 9

Make the Sweet Pie Dough as described on page 20 but just before refrigerating it, divide it in half; one part should be slightly bigger than the other. Shape each portion into a disc, wrap in clingfilm/plastic wrap and refrigerate it for at least 1 hour, and up to 2 days. If you're in a hurry you can chill the larger portion of dough in the freezer for 15 minutes and the smaller one just until you're ready to use it. If refrigerated, allow the dough to rest at room temperature for 5–10 minutes before rolling it out.

Preheat the oven to 180°C (350°F) Gas 4.

Cut out a piece of parchment paper to fit the base of the baking pan. Dust with a little flour and place the larger portion of dough on it, then dust the dough with flour. Roll out with a rolling pin, from the centre outwards, until it's roughly the size of the base of the pan. Brush off any excess flour and transfer the dough, together with the paper, into the pan. If necessary, use a glass to roll out the dough so that it covers the entire base of the pan. Prick all over with a fork and bake in the preheated oven for 6–7 minutes. Leave the oven on.

For the filling, grate the apples by hand with a grater, or core them and use a food processor to grate them. If the apples are very juicy, squeeze out some of the juice to prevent it seeping into the dough and making it soggy. Mix the apples with the raisins, syrup and cinnamon, then spread over the half-baked base with a spatula.

Take the smaller portion of dough and grate by hand with a grater. Scatter it evenly over the apple filling. Put back in the oven and bake for 25–35 minutes, until the top is golden and the base is also nice and golden (lift the paper with a spatula to check this).

Allow to cool in the pan before serving. Store in an airtight container for a couple of days.

I was surprised to find so many different types of cheesecake around the world! Some are unbaked, some are baked; some are fruit flavoured, others contain chocolate. My vegan cheesecake is baked and apricot flavoured, with a pie crust, and it looks beautiful!

Apricot and tofu cheesecake

½ quantity Sweet Pie Dough (page 20)

FOR THE TOFU CREAM

500 g/1 lb. 2 oz. plain, medium-soft tofu

100 g/scant ½ cup vanilla soy custard

1½ tablespoons non-hydrogenated margarine

85 g/⅓ cup rice or agave syrup

freshly squeezed juice of 1½ lemons

grated zest of 2 lemons

1 tablespoon unbleached plain/all-purpose flour

4-5 ripe firm apricots (if in season), pitted and sliced

FOR THE APRICOT JELLY

1 teaspoon agar powder or 2 teaspoons agar flakes

110 ml/½ cup apple concentrate

135 g/½ cup smooth, naturally sweetened apricot jam

28-cm/11-in. springform cake pan or loose-based tart pan

Serves 6-8

Make and refrigerate the Sweet Pie Dough as described on page 20.

For the tofu cream, blanch the tofu in boiling water for 2 minutes. Put it in a food processor with the custard, margarine, syrup, lemon juice and zest, and flour. Blend until smooth.

Preheat the oven to 180°C (350°F) Gas 4.

Take the dough out of the fridge. Place it between 2 sheets of parchment paper and use a rolling pin to roll the dough out to a circle about 31 cm/13 inches in diameter. Loosely roll the dough circle around the rolling pin and unroll it over the tart pan. Neatly line the pan with the dough and trim off any excess from the edges with a pastry wheel or your fingers. Patch up any holes with dough off-cuts. Prick the base all over with a fork and bake in the preheated oven for 8–10 minutes. Leave the oven on.

Remove the pan from the oven and pour the tofu cream into the tart crust. Spread level with a spatula. Put back in the oven and bake for 20 minutes, or until the tofu cream starts turning very lightly golden. Allow to cool completely in the pan. Arrange the apricot slices over the cooled tofu cream, if using.

For the apricot jelly, put 285 ml/1¼ cups water, the agar, apple concentrate and jam in a saucepan and bring to the boil, whisking occasionally. Lower the heat and cook for 2 minutes if you are using agar powder, or 8 minutes if using flakes or until the flakes have completely melted.

Gently ladle the hot jelly over the cooled cheesecake but if you think it will leak over the edges, only ladle some of it in, then wait for 3–4 minutes to firm slightly before adding the rest. Allow to cool completely. This is best done in the fridge.

Cut into slices with a sharp knife dipped in hot water.

When peaches are in season, I can eat huge amounts of them every day, but instead of eating them raw all the time, I use them to bake fancy summer desserts once in a while. It's especially nice to serve this crumble on a stormy summer evening when there is a bit of rain and wind and everybody feels very shivery and miserable even though it's summertime!

Peach crumble

1.8 kg/about 8 firm but ripe peaches
2-3 tablespoons apple juice concentrate
1 tablespoon unbleached plain/all-purpose flour
a pinch of salt

FOR THE CRUMBLE
80 g/½ cup hazelnuts or other nuts
65 g/½ cup unbleached plain/all-purpose flour
50 g/½ cup rolled oats
grated zest of 1 orange or lemon
¼ teaspoon ground cinnamon
⅛ teaspoon bourbon vanilla powder
a pinch of salt
85 g/⅓ cup brown rice or agave syrup
50 g/⅓ cup non-hydrogenated margarine, at room temperature

ovenproof dish, 8-cup capacity

Serves 6–8

Preheat the oven to 150°C (300°F) Gas 2.

For the crumble, put the nuts in a baking pan and roast in the preheated oven for 8–10 minutes. Rub off any skins that have loosened from the nuts, then roughly chop the nuts by hand or in a food processor. Big pieces will burn while the crumble is baking, so make them quite small.

Put the flour, oats, zest, cinnamon, vanilla powder and salt in a bowl and stir. Add the syrup and mix well, then work the margarine in with your hands, rubbing it quickly between your fingers. When the mixture looks crumbly, add the chopped nuts.

Preheat the oven to 180°C (350°F) Gas 4.

Blanch the peaches in a saucepan of boiling water for 1–2 minutes – just long enough to be able to peel the skin off easily. Transfer them to a bowl of cold water so you don't burn your fingers, then peel off the skin. Halve and pit the peaches and cut them into wedges. Toss them with the apple juice concentrate, flour and salt. Spread them in the ovenproof dish and cover them evenly with the crumble.

Bake in the preheated oven for about 35 minutes or until the crumble topping is golden brown and the juice is bubbling up around the edges.

The crumble is best served warm, but if you happen to have leftovers and serve it as a dessert the next day, I'm sure no one will complain!

Here is a very rustic-looking, freeform tart that I cannot resist eating more of than I should! Using non-hydrogenated margarine in this type of dough is a little tricky; it will result in a healthier dessert that will impress with its taste but maybe not with its looks! If you prefer it to be prettier, use shortening instead. I love it just the way it is.

Plum crostata

3 tablespoons pure maple syrup, for brushing

FOR THE CRUST (SEE METHOD BEFORE STARTING)

100 g/¾ cup unbleached plain/all-purpose flour

65 g/½ cup plain wholemeal/whole-wheat flour

¼ teaspoon salt

70 g/½ cup non-hydrogenated margarine

1 tablespoon pure maple syrup

ice-cold water, if needed

FOR THE FILLING

350 g/12 oz. small plums, eg. Italian prune plums

2 tablespoons naturally sweetened plum (or other) jam

grated zest of 1 lemon

2 tablespoons pure maple syrup (optional)

35 g/⅓ cup ground almonds or other nuts

¼ teaspoon ground cinnamon

Serves 4–5

For the crust, refrigerate all the ingredients (but freeze the margarine) for 30 minutes before starting.

After 30 minutes, put the flours and salt in a bowl and stir. Gradually add small pieces of margarine to the bowl and using a fork (or a food processor), mix them in until the ingredients look crumbly. Add the syrup and mix in with a spatula. Now check – if the dough just holds together, it's ready. If it's too dry, add 1 teaspoon ice-cold water, mix in and check again. You should get a dough that is not falling apart but isn't sticky or moist. Don't overwork it and don't handle it too much.

Shape the dough into a disc, wrap in clingfilm/plastic wrap and refrigerate it for at least 1 hour, and up to 3 days.

Meanwhile, for the filling, pit and quarter the plums. Mix them with the jam, zest and syrup, if using.

Preheat the oven to 180°C (350°F) Gas 4.

Take the dough out of the fridge. Place it between 2 sheets of parchment paper and use a rolling pin to roll the dough out to a circle about 28 cm/11 inches in diameter. Discard the top sheet of paper. Transfer the dough, together with the bottom sheet of paper, to a baking sheet. Sprinkle the ground almonds and cinnamon evenly over the dough. Spoon the filling over this, leaving a 4-cm/1¾-inch border. Fold the border over to encase the filling around the edge. Do this gently, and if the dough crumbles or cracks a little, don't worry, just try to patch it up by pressing lightly with your fingertips. It will come together during baking. Brush maple syrup around the edge of the crostata and bake in the preheated oven for 25–30 minutes.

Allow to cool completely on the baking sheet before cutting into slices to serve.

Not all baked desserts must have baked fillings. Why not contrast the crumbly crust with some fresh, raw fruit for extra freshness and flavour? Made with olive oil, these tartlets are quite light, and the crust is neutral so it can be used to make savoury tartlets as well. Using a muffin pan to bake them is very practical, so you don't need to buy mini-tart pans just for this recipe!

Fresh fruit tartlets

fresh mint, melissa or mini-basil leaves, for decoration
pure maple syrup, for drizzling

FOR THE CRUST

215 g/1⅔ cups unbleached plain/all-purpose flour
2 tablespoons fine cornmeal
½ teaspoon baking powder
¼ teaspoon sea salt
100 g/½ cup olive oil
1 teaspoon lemon juice
1 tablespoon ice-cold water

FOR THE FILLING

300 g/10 oz. seasonal fruits, (the combination of apricots and nectarines is nice)
140 g/½ cup naturally sweetened apricot jam
¼ teaspoon bourbon vanilla powder
1 teaspoon rum or mirin
a pinch of salt
8 tablespoons vanilla soy custard (optional)

muffin pan

Makes 8 tartlets

For the crust, sift together the flour, cornmeal, baking powder and salt in a bowl. Whisk in the oil, lemon juice and ice-cold water. Knead the dough for a few seconds, just until it holds together. Add a couple more drops of water if it seems too dry. Wrap in clingfilm/plastic wrap and refrigerate for at least 1 hour.

Meanwhile, for the filling, slice or chop the fruit into small pieces and mix them with the jam, vanilla powder, rum and salt.

Preheat the oven to 180°C (350°F) Gas 4.

Take the dough out of the fridge. Divide into 8 equal portions and place each in a hole of the muffin pan. Press and pat the dough gently to line the base and reach halfway up the sides. Make sure the layer of dough in the base is quite thin as it rises a bit during baking, and you will want some space inside the tartlet case later for the fruit. Prick the base of each case with a fork and bake in the preheated oven for 12–15 minutes, or until lightly golden. Do not overbake. Allow to cool completely before carefully turning the cases out of the pan with a spatula or a small knife.

Just before serving, put a tablespoon of custard, if using, inside each tartlet case and top with as much fruit as it can take. Decorate with fresh herbs and drizzle over and around with maple syrup.

Ganache is usually made with cream but I use soft tofu instead and the result is smooth and rich, making a great tart filling. I created this recipe with serious chocoholics in mind, adding chocolate mousse on top of the ganache.

Chocolate ganache tart

½ quantity Sweet Pie Dough (page 20)

FOR THE GANACHE
620 g/1 lb. 6 oz. plain, soft tofu
390 g/3 cups finely chopped vegan dark/bittersweet chocolate (70% cocoa)
grated zest of 2½ lemons
brown rice syrup or other sweetener, to taste
non-dairy milk or cream, if needed

FOR THE MOUSSE
450 ml/2 cups chocolate soy or oat milk
160 g/1¼ cups finely chopped vegan dark/bittersweet chocolate (70% cocoa)
85 g/⅓ cup brown rice syrup
90 g/7 tablespoons cornflour/cornstarch

28-cm/11-in. springform cake pan or loose-based tart pan

Serves 6–8

Make and refrigerate the Sweet Pie Dough as described on page 20.

For the ganache, blanch the tofu in boiling water for 2 minutes. Meanwhile, melt the chocolate in a heatproof bowl set over a saucepan of simmering water. Do not let the base of the bowl touch the water. Put the blanched tofu, melted chocolate and lemon zest in food processor. Blend until smooth. Taste and if it's not sweet enough, blend in syrup to taste; if too thick, add a little milk or cream while blending.

Preheat the oven to 180°C (350°F) Gas 4.

Take the dough out of the fridge. Place it between 2 sheets of parchment paper and use a rolling pin to roll the dough out to a circle about 31 cm/13 inches in diameter. Loosely roll the dough circle around the rolling pin and unroll it over the tart pan. Neatly line the pan with the dough and trim off any excess from the edges with a pastry wheel or your fingers. Patch up any holes with dough off-cuts. Prick the base all over with a fork and bake in the preheated oven for 8–10 minutes. Leave the oven on.

Remove the pan from the oven and pour the ganache into the tart crust. Spread level with a spatula. Put back in the oven and bake for 15 minutes or until the edges turn lightly golden. Allow to cool completely in the pan.

For the mousse, heat the chocolate milk in a saucepan, then add the chocolate and syrup and whisk until the chocolate has melted. Mix the cornflour/cornstarch into 5–6 tablespoons water. Slowly add this to the saucepan over low heat, whisking vigorously. Keep whisking and it will start to thicken once it reaches the right temperature. Allow to cool slightly.

Spread the mousse over the cold ganache in the tart case with the spatula. Refrigerate but allow to come to room temperature for 20 minutes before serving. Cut into slices with a sharp knife dipped in hot water.

Fruit strudels are wonderful! Made healthily with little oil and healthy sweeteners, they can be eaten as a dessert, for breakfast, packed in lunchboxes or picnic baskets. This is a nice autumn combination of sweet pears and untreated (unsulfured) dried apricots with a touch of rum, vanilla and citrus aroma.

Aromatic pear strudel

500 g/1 lb. 2 oz./10 large sheets of filo/phyllo pastry

125 g/15 unsulfured dried apricots, chopped

2 tablespoons rum or mirin

2 teaspoons vanilla extract

freshly squeezed juice and grated zest of 2 lemons or oranges

a pinch of salt

8 ripe pears, eg. Abate

85 g/⅓ cup apple juice concentrate or pure maple syrup

65 g/¼ cup coconut oil mixed with 4 tablespoons water

40 x 28-cm/16 x 11-in. baking pan, lightly oiled

Makes 20 slices

Take the filo/phyllo sheets out of the fridge 30 minutes before making the strudel. This will prevent the sheets from cracking during baking.

Meanwhile, put the apricots in a bowl with the rum, vanilla extract, lemon juice and zest and allow to soak while you prepare the pears, or longer if possible.

Preheat the oven to 180°C (350°F) Gas 4.

Peel and core the pears. Cut them into small cubes and mix them with the soaked apricots and the apple concentrate or syrup. Divide the mixture into 5 equal portions.

Place a sheet of filo/phyllo on a dry work surface with the longer side facing you. (Cover the remaining sheets with clingfilm/plastic wrap to prevent them from drying out.) Brush the coconut-oil mixture lightly over the sheet. Cover it with another sheet (this one doesn't need oiling).

Spread one portion of pears lengthwise along the bottom edge of the sheet. Arrange them in a 6-cm/2½-inch-wide strip, leaving a 2-cm/¾-inch edge on each side to prevent the filling from spilling out. Roll the sheet up carefully around the filling and into a nice strudel and place in the baking pan. Repeat with the remaining sheets and filling to get 5 strudels in the pan. Brush them lightly with the coconut-oil mixture and use a sharp knife to score each strudel into 4 slices.

Bake the strudel in the preheated oven for 25–30 minutes or until golden.

Serve warm or cold. It will keep in an airtight container in the fridge for up to 3 days and should be reheated in the oven before serving. Serve it with vegan vanilla custard and you'll be adored by your family and guests!

This is a vegan version of a traditional dessert from the northern border between Croatia and Slovenia, originally called 'gibanica'.

Apple, poppy-seed and walnut pie

500 g/1 lb. 2 oz./12 sheets of filo/phyllo pastry

100 g/½ cup sunflower oil

FOR THE POPPY-SEED LAYER

400 ml/1¾ cups non-dairy milk

200 g/2⅓ cups ground poppy seeds (available online)

5 tablespoons brown rice syrup

40 g/3 tablespoons raisins

¼ teaspoon bourbon vanilla powder

1 tablespoon rum

grated zest of 1 lemon

FOR THE TOFU LAYER

400 g/14 oz. fresh, plain, medium-soft tofu

2 tablespoons arrowroot powder or cornflour/cornstarch

110 ml/½ cup non-dairy milk

55 ml/⅓ cup lemon juice

3 tablespoons brown rice syrup

FOR THE WALNUT LAYER

200 g/1¼ cups walnuts

30 g/⅓ cup fine breadcrumbs

5 tablespoons brown rice syrup

230 ml/1 cup non-dairy milk

FOR THE APPLE LAYER

500 g/1 lb. 2 oz. tart apples

40 g/3 tablespoons raisins

¼ teaspoon ground cinnamon

2 tablespoons brown rice syrup

juice of ½ lemon

20 x 30-cm/8 x 12-in. baking pan, well oiled

Makes 12 squares

For the poppy-seed layer, boil the milk and pour it over the remaining ingredients. Mix well and cover until ready to use.

For the tofu layer, crumble the tofu with your fingers. Dilute the arrowroot in a little milk, then whisk together all the ingredients.

For the walnut layer, finely grind the walnuts in a spice mill. Mix with the breadcrumbs and syrup. Boil the milk and pour it over the walnut mixture. Cover until ready to use.

For the apple layer, peel and grate the apples by hand with a grater, or core them and use a food processor to grate them. Combine with the remaining ingredients.

Preheat the oven to 180°C (350°F) Gas 4.

If the sheets of filo/phyllo are bigger than your baking pan, cut them to size. Don't worry if a sheet tears as you can easily patch up any damage – only the top 3 sheets need to stay undamaged.

Place a sheet of filo/phyllo in the baking pan. (Cover the remaining sheets with clingfilm/plastic wrap to prevent them from drying out.) Brush oil lightly over the sheet. Cover with another sheet and oil it. Cover with a third sheet (this one doesn't need oiling). Spread the poppy-seed layer evenly over the top with a spatula. Cover with one sheet, oil lightly and cover with a second sheet. Spread the tofu layer on top. Cover with one sheet, oil lightly and cover with a second sheet. Spread the walnut layer on top (but if the mixture has soaked up all the milk, just sprinkle it). Cover with one sheet, oil lightly and cover with a second sheet. Spread the apple layer on top. Brush a little oil over the remaining 3 undamaged sheets and lay them on top of the pie. Brush a little more oil on the top sheet. Tuck in any pastry or filling sticking out of the pan by pushing a spatula between the pie and the sides of the pan. Use a sharp knife to score 12 squares into the pastry.

Bake in the preheated oven for 45–50 minutes, or until the top turns golden brown and the pie isn't wobbly or soft to the touch. Allow to cool completely (at least 5 hours, or overnight) in the pan before serving. It tastes much better when left to soak up the juices.

If you still haven't heard of this dessert of Turkish origin, you are missing out! Baklava is one of those really sweet desserts that you can't eat a lot of. It's a bit of work to make it, but it can be made in advance and requires only four basic ingredients: filo/phyllo sheets, nuts, sweetener and oil. This allows you to play with different types of nuts and sweeteners and create your favourite baklava without fear of messing up.

Healthier baklava rolls

100 g/½ cup sunflower oil

600 g/1 lb. 5 oz./20 sheets of filo/phyllo pastry

FOR THE SYRUP

390 g/1½ cups agave or pure maple syrup, or to taste

½ teaspoon bourbon vanilla powder

2 lemons

FOR THE FILLING

500 g/4½ cups walnuts

120 g/¾ cup semolina/farina

100 g/½ cup Demerara sugar

1 teaspoon baking powder

40 x 28-cm/16 x 11-in. baking pan

Serves 12

Preheat the oven to 180°C (350°F) Gas 4.

For the syrup, put the syrup and vanilla powder in a saucepan with 560 ml/2½ cups water and heat until boiling. Cut one of the lemons in half, then cut one half into slices and add them to the syrup. Lower the heat, cover and cook for a few minutes. Remove from the heat and stir in the juice and zest of the remaining 1½ lemons. Allow to cool completely.

For the filling, grind the walnuts in a spice mill, then mix well with the remaining ingredients.

Mix 50 ml/¼ cup water with 60 ml/¼ cup of the oil.

Place a sheet of filo/phyllo on a dry work surface with the longer side facing you. (Cover the remaining sheets with clingfilm/plastic wrap to prevent them from drying out.) Brush the oil mixture lightly over the sheet. Cover with another sheet (this one doesn't need oiling).

Take one-tenth of the filling and spread it lengthwise along the bottom edge of the sheet, leaving a 2-cm/¾-inch edge on each side to prevent the filling from spilling out. Roll the sheet up tightly around the filling and into a nice sausage. Repeat this with the remaining sheets of filo/phyllo and the filling. You should have 10 rolls of baklava. Arrange them snugly in the baking pan. Use a sharp knife to score each roll into 5–6 smaller rolls and brush them with the remaining oil.

Bake in the preheated oven until golden brown. Check if the bottoms of the rolls are baked too before taking the pan out of the oven. Pour the syrup evenly over all the rolls.

Allow to cool completely (at least 2 hours, or overnight) in the pan before serving to allow the baklava to soak up the syrup. It will keep in an airtight container in the fridge for up to 1 week.

CHAPTER 6

Breads and savoury baking

For breakfast, lunch or dinner – in fact at any time of day – what people most often crave is a piece of bread with their meal. From the simplest, quickest loaf, to a proper focaccia, via other savoury bakes such as corn and tofu pie, and rye and olive-oil crackers, this chapter will inspire you to get creative with your vegan savoury baking.

Many of my friends admire my baking skills because I bake fresh bread for my clients almost every day. But after I share this recipe with them, the looks of admiration in their eyes fade slightly when they realize how ridiculously easy it is to bake! Honestly, no special skills are required to make this crisp-crusted loaf with a chewy inside. Just follow the recipe and you'll do just fine!

No-knead everyday bread

330 g/2¾ cups unbleached plain/all-purpose flour

2 teaspoons baking powder

60 g/½ cup plain wholemeal/whole-wheat flour

50 g/½ cup fine rolled oats

12 g/1½ teaspoons salt

240 ml/1 cup plain soy yogurt (thinner kind, if available)

225 ml/1 cup sparkling mineral water

2 tablespoons olive oil

FOR THE SEED MIX

2 tablespoons rolled oats

½ teaspoon caraway seeds

2 tablespoons sesame or other seeds

500-g/1-lb. loaf pan

oven thermometer (optional)

Makes about 8 slices

Preheat the oven to 220°C (425°F) Gas 7.

Sift together the unbleached flour and baking powder, then stir in the wholemeal/whole-wheat flour, oats and salt and mix well.

In a separate bowl, mix together the yogurt, water and oil. Pour into the dry ingredients, mixing vigorously with a wooden spoon until you get a sticky dough with no flour left on the bottom of the bowl. The dough should be easy to spoon. If it's very thick and sticky, add 1–2 more tablespoons sparkling mineral water.

In order to get a nicely shaped loaf, cut a sheet of parchment paper to fit inside the loaf pan without any creases. For the seed mix, combine the oats, caraway seeds and sesame seeds, then sprinkle half over the base of the loaf pan. Spoon the dough into the pan, spread level with a wet spatula and top with the remaining seed mix. Press it gently into the dough with the wet spatula.

Put the bread in the preheated oven, lower the temperature to 200°C (400°F) Gas 6 and bake for 1 hour. Use an oven thermometer if you're not sure about the exact temperature in the oven. If you notice that the top of the bread is browning after 40 minutes, cover with a piece of parchment paper and continue baking.

Remove from the oven, allow to cool in the pan for 10 minutes, then tip the bread out of the pan, peel off the paper and allow to cool completely on a wire rack. This will prevent the bread from absorbing moisture and will keep the crust crisp.

Store the bread wrapped in a kitchen towel in a cool, dry place for up to 5 days.

I tried many different pizza and focaccia dough recipes: with baking powder, the old-fashioned way with fresh yeast, etc., but I got the best results ever when making it as explained in the recipe below. It's true that you need a few hours for the dough to rise, but it's worth every minute! I just do a lot of other stuff while the yeast is working its magic...

Herb focaccia

**Pizza and Focaccia Dough
(page 20)**

**4 teaspoons dried herbs of your
choice, eg. rosemary,
oregano (or fennel seeds)**

**1 teaspoon coarse sea salt
(Himalayan, if available)**

*23 x 30 cm/9 x 12-in. baking
pan, well oiled*

Serves 6

Make the Pizza and Focaccia Dough as described on page 20 and allow to rise for 2½ hours in a warm place.

After 2½ hours, shape the dough to fit the prepared baking pan by gently pressing and pushing it from the middle toward the edges. Make dimples by poking the dough with your fingertips. Drizzle with olive oil, cover and allow to rise again for 2 hours. Do not skip this step as the end result will be a much tougher bread without this second rising.

Preheat the oven to 180°C (350°F) Gas 4.

Sprinkle the dried herbs of your choice and the salt over the dough. Bake in the preheated oven for 20 minutes, or until golden and crisp.

Remove from the oven and allow to cool slightly in the pan before cutting into squares.

Focaccia is great with stews and soups but can also be served on any occasion for which you would serve bread. Focaccia sandwiches are exceptionally popular with my family and friends; I cut one focaccia into 6 equal pieces, then slice each piece in half through the middle. I spread tofu mayo or hummus on the bottom half, top with marinated fried or baked tofu, seitan or tempeh and add as many vegetables, pickles, sprouts and greens as I can fit inside. It's a complete meal in itself – very nutritious and very filling.

It's so easy to make crackers that I sometimes wonder why people spend so much money buying them. All you need is 20 minutes to make a batch that will always be so much healthier and taste exactly as you like! I've reduced the quantity of salt in my crackers to a minimum, since I usually serve them with some kind of spicy spread or dip, but if you plan to eat them as a snack, you can add another ⅛ teaspoon of salt to the dough.

Rye and olive oil crackers

130 g/¾ cup rye flour

130 g/¾ cup unbleached plain/all-purpose flour

2 tablespoons unhulled sesame seeds

½ teaspoon salt

freshly ground black pepper, to taste

50 g/¼ cup olive oil

1 teaspoon brown rice syrup

baking sheet, lined with parchment paper

Makes about 16

Mix together the flours, seeds, salt and some pepper in a bowl.

In a separate bowl, whisk together the oil, 60 ml/¼ cup water and the syrup to emulsify. Slowly pour into the bowl of dry ingredients, stirring until well combined. The dough should quickly form a ball and shouldn't be sticky. Knead a couple of times, just enough to make sure all the ingredients are evenly distributed. Wrap the dough in clingfilm/plastic wrap and allow to rest at room temperature for 10 minutes. This will make rolling out the dough much easier.

Divide the dough into 3 equal portions.

Preheat the oven to 200°C (400°F) Gas 6.

Place the dough between 2 sheets of parchment paper and use a rolling pin to roll it out very thinly. If you like really crunchy crackers, the dough should be almost paper-thin, but if you like a bit of texture, roll it to your preferred thickness.

Use a knife or a pizza cutter to cut out shapes; squares or rectangles are most practical, as you'll have hardly any leftover dough. Re-roll any trimmings. Transfer the crackers to the prepared baking sheet using a spatula or thin knife. Prick each one a couple of times with a fork.

Bake in the preheated oven for 4–7 minutes, depending on the thickness of the crackers. Remember that they shouldn't brown, just get slightly golden. They will firm up as they cool, so don't expect them to be cracker-crunchy straight out of the oven!

Allow to cool completely and then store in an airtight container for about 1–2 weeks.

There are so many ways to make cornbread and I realized that many people expect it to be sweet, like cake. This one is not a corn 'cake', even though the texture does resemble cake a little. It's a mild bread that I serve with stews, rich salads or soups. I love to eat it on its own too, as a snack when I travel or go for a day trip to the countryside. For the best results, use finely ground yellow cornmeal and a little coarse cornmeal/polenta for sprinkling – it gives the cornbread a good crust.

25-minute cornbread

200 g/1½ cups fine cornmeal

200 g/1½ cups unbleached plain/all-purpose flour

1 teaspoon baking powder

½ teaspoon bicarbonate of/baking soda

1 teaspoon salt

450 ml/2 cups plain soy milk

75 ml/⅓ cup sparkling mineral water

1 tablespoon apple cider vinegar

2 tablespoons brown rice syrup or other sweetener

2 tablespoons sunflower oil

2 tablespoons coarse cornmeal/polenta

23 x 30 cm/9 x 12-in. baking pan, well oiled

Makes 12–15 slices

Preheat the oven to 180°C (350°F) Gas 4.

Sift together the cornmeal, flour, baking powder, bicarbonate of/baking soda and salt.

In a separate bowl, whisk together the milk, water, vinegar, syrup and oil. Pour into the bowl of dry ingredients and combine them to get a smooth batter but do not overmix.

Pour the batter into the prepared baking pan and spread level with a spatula. Sprinkle the coarse cornmeal/polenta over the bread.

Bake in the preheated oven for 25 minutes, or until the bread starts to turn golden and the corners begin to shrink from the sides of the pan. Be careful not to overbake it!

Allow to cool completely in the pan. Store in an airtight container or wrapped in a kitchen towel for up to 5 days.

Grissini are a great snack and a very popular party food. Why many people are reluctant to make them at home, I really don't know. They're so easy! They can be served on their own, with a dip, with soup – the possibilities are numerous and the enjoyment is guaranteed. When my friend Melani was moving into her new apartment, I tied a portion of long grissini with natural raffia strings and gave her this 'bouquet' instead of flowers! Do I need to add that we ate them all right away?

Grissini with caraway seeds

140 ml/⅔ cup lukewarm water

5 g/1 teaspoon active dry yeast (additive-free)

1 teaspoon barley malt or other sweetener

190 g/1½ cups strong unbleached bread flour

30 g/¼ cup strong wholemeal/ whole-wheat bread flour

30 g/¼ cup fine cornmeal

½ teaspoon salt

½ teaspoon caraway seeds

3 tablespoons olive oil

baking sheets, lined with parchment paper

Makes 20 long grissini

Whisk the water, yeast and barley malt together in a small bowl, cover and allow to rest for 15 minutes. The yeast will start to foam slightly while it is resting.

In a separate bowl, mix the flours, cornmeal, salt, caraway seeds and 2 tablespoons of the oil. Add the bubbly yeast mixture and mix until it comes together. Transfer to a lightly floured surface and knead until smooth – about 4 minutes. Place on a prepared baking sheet and, using a silicone spatula, rub oil lightly over the dough. Put in the oven with only the light on and allow to rise for 1 hour.

After 1 hour, preheat the oven to 180°C (350°F) Gas 4.

Take the dough out of the oven and shape it into a flat oval shape. Using a sharp, wide knife, cut the dough into strips 1 cm/½ inch wide. Pull and stretch each strip into a long stick. Some strips will be longer and thicker so you'll be able to stretch 2 or 3 grissini out of them. You should get about 20 grissini roughly 35 cm/14 inches long. They puff up a little while baking. I never use a rolling pin to stretch them as that flattens them too much and pushes out the air which results in tough grissini.

Place the stretched grissini back on the prepared baking sheets spaced 7 mm/⅓ inch apart. Brush a little oil over each one and bake in the preheated oven, in batches, for 12–15 minutes, turning the grissini over halfway through baking.

Allow to cool on the baking sheets and store in a sealed bag for about 10 days.

This is my version of a recipe that dates way back to the time of the Turkish invasions of the Adriatic coast. Traditionally it was baked as a huge circular pie over coals, but since modern families often have four members or fewer and live in tiny city apartments, a recipe for small pies baked in the oven makes much more sense! It's a great lunch that is light yet satisfying, rich in fibre (from the wholemeal/whole-wheat and rye flours), without any raising agents and filled with vegetables.

Soparnik pies with onions and greens

100 g/¾ cup wholemeal/
   whole-wheat flour
65 g/½ cup rye flour
¼ teaspoon salt
2 tablespoons olive oil

FOR THE FILLING
180 g/6½ oz. tender chard
½ small onion
2 garlic cloves
2 tablespoons olive oil
salt and freshly ground black
   pepper, to taste

Serves 1–2

Preheat the oven to 180°C (350°F) Gas 4.

Mix together the flours and salt, then add the oil and rub it in. Slowly add cold water (up to 55 ml/¼ cup) to get a firm dough that doesn't stick to the work surface when you knead it briefly. Wrap the dough in clingfilm/plastic wrap and allow to rest at room temperature while you prepare the filling.

For the filling, remove any particularly large and tough stems from the chard. Wash, pat dry with a kitchen towel and thinly slice. Add a pinch of salt to the chopped chard in a bowl and massage in for a minute, or until it begins to wilt. Pat dry with a kitchen towel again. This way, the pie won't turn out soggy.

Finely chop the onion and garlic and add to the wilted chard together with the oil and season with salt and pepper.

Divide the rested dough in half. Put a sheet of parchment paper down and put one portion of dough on it. Roll out with a rolling pin into a circle about 18 cm/7 inches in diameter. Spoon the filling onto the dough circle, leaving a 1-cm/¼-inch border without filling. Roll out the other portion of dough in the same way, prick with a fork and lay over the filling. Seal the pie by folding over the edge of the dough all the way around the circle and pressing together with your fingers. Crimp into a scalloped edge, if you like.

Slide the pie and paper onto a baking sheet and put in the preheated oven. The raw dough is quite dark but you will notice that the top and bottom will turn golden after 22–24 minutes. At this point, remove the pie from the oven and allow to cool slightly.

Serve warm with some soy yogurt, or cool completely, store in an airtight container and take anywhere you might need a nutritious light meal!

It's always useful to bake some good-quality snacks in advance and have them stored for emergencies! Homemade snacks are always 150 per cent healthier than anything you can buy in the supermarkets or your local store, so why snack on oily chips, processed and additive-rich pretzels, sticks, etc. when you can make your own tasty bites for the whole family to enjoy?

Cracker snacks with black sesame seeds

260 g/2 cups flour of your choice, or a combination of 2–3 different kinds, if you like, chilled (yes, chilled!)

¼ teaspoon salt

4 teaspoons baking powder

140 g/1 cup non-hydrogenated margarine, chilled

1 tablespoon brown rice syrup

50 ml/¼ cup ice-cold plain soy milk or water, or as needed

FOR THE TOPPING

black sesame seeds (or other seeds like sesame, caraway, cumin, dried oregano, dried basil etc.)

coarse sea salt

Makes lots!

Put the flour, salt and baking powder in a food processor and pulse to mix. Add the margarine and pulse 6–8 times until the mixture resembles coarse breadcrumbs. Add the syrup and pulse again a couple of times. Gradually add the ice-cold milk or water 1 tablespoon at a time, pulsing until the mixture just begins to clump together. If you pinch some of the crumbly dough and it holds together, it's ready. If the dough doesn't hold together, add a little more liquid and pulse again. Be careful not to add too much otherwise it will make the crackers tough.

Place the dough on a lightly floured work surface. Knead it just enough to form a ball but do not over-knead it. Shape it into a disc, wrap it in clingfilm/plastic wrap and refrigerate it for at least 1 hour, and up to 2 days. If you're in a hurry you can chill the dough in the freezer for 15 minutes. Allow the dough to rest at room temperature for about 5–10 minutes before rolling it out.

Preheat the oven to 180°C (350°F) Gas 4.

Place the dough on a sheet of lightly floured parchment paper, dust with a little flour and roll it out with a rolling pin until 1 mm/1⁄32 inch thick. Use a pastry wheel to cut it into short or long sticks, or you could stamp out shapes with a cookie cutter. Slide the crackers and paper onto a baking sheet. Separate each cracker so they don't stick together while cooking.

For the topping, lightly brush each cracker with water and sprinkle the black sesame seeds over the top. Salt lightly.

Bake in the preheated oven for 10 minutes, or until the dough puffs up a little and turns golden. Allow to cool completely on the baking sheet. Store in an airtight container for up to 2 weeks.

This is one of my favourite lunches during pumpkin season, served with a big bowl of salad and a cup of non-dairy yogurt. It's important to roll the dough really thinly to get snails that are slightly crunchy but still melt in your mouth. I love to use a small amount of onion in the filling as well, but you can omit it if you want.

Pastry snails with spicy pumpkin filling

180 g/1⅓ cups unbleached plain/all-purpose flour

¼ teaspoon salt

3 tablespoons sunflower oil

FOR THE FILLING

200 g/2 cups grated pumpkin, eg. Hokkaido or other dense-fleshed pumpkin

½ onion, finely chopped

½ teaspoon tamari soy sauce

2 garlic cloves, crushed

¼ teaspoon salt

1 tablespoon olive oil, plus extra for brushing

½ teaspoon ground ginger

1 teaspoon lemon juice

freshly ground black pepper, to taste

baking sheet, lined with parchment paper

Makes 8

Preheat the oven to 180°C (350°F) Gas 4.

Mix together the flour and salt, then add the oil and rub it in. Slowly add cold water (up to 80 ml/⅓ cup) to get a dough that doesn't stick to the work surface when you try to knead it. Wrap the dough in clingfilm/plastic wrap and allow to rest at room temperature while you prepare the filling.

For the filling, mix together all the ingredients with your hands or a wooden spoon. Divide it into 8 equal portions.

Divide the dough again into 4 equal portions. While you are working with one, keep the others wrapped in clingfilm/plastic wrap to prevent them drying out. Put one portion of dough on a sheet of parchment paper, dust with a little flour and shape the dough into a small log with your hands. Roll it out with a rolling pin, as thinly as you can, into a square. The sheet of dough should be almost see-through. Trim any uneven edges, then cut in half to make 2 equal rectangles. These will make 2 snails.

Spread one portion of filling along the bottom edge of the rectangle. Roll the rectangle up carefully around the filling and into a nice, tight sausage. Bend it into a spiral/snail shape. Seal the edge by wetting your finger and pressing it gently but firmly against the snail. Tuck the end neatly underneath the snail. Repeat with the remaining sheets and filling to get 8 snails.

Arrange the snails on the prepared baking sheet and brush them lightly with oil. Bake in the preheated oven for about 35–40 minutes until golden.

Allow to cool slightly (or completely), then serve plain or brushed with a little more oil and soy sauce if you prefer them to be saltier. These snails are great as a portable meal too – very practical!

A vegan version of Greek filo/phyllo pie, this dish makes an excellent lunch or dinner and is very filling. Corn kernels add a nice sweetness and texture to the smooth tofu layers, but using some blanched greens instead of corn is also a delicious variation worth trying. Serve with a big bowl of salad, or a cup of non-dairy yogurt if you're in a hurry.

Corn and tofu pie

500 g/1 lb. 2 oz./17 sheets of filo/phyllo pastry
100 g/½ cup olive oil

FOR THE FILLING
250 g/2 cups corn kernels, fresh, canned, or frozen and thawed
500 g/1 lb. 2 oz. plain, medium-soft tofu
2 tablespoons olive oil
2¼ teaspoons salt
460 ml/2 cups plain soy milk
230 ml/1 cup hot water
130 g/1 cup fine cornmeal

20 x 30-cm/8 x 12-in. baking pan, well oiled

Serves 6–8

If using canned corn, wash it and drain well. In a big bowl, crumble the tofu with your fingers and add the corn, oil, salt, milk and hot water and mix until well combined. Whisk in the cornmeal. The filling should be moderately smooth besides the corn and small pieces of tofu.

Preheat the oven to 180°C (350°F) Gas 4.

If the sheets of filo/phyllo are bigger than your baking pan, cut them to size. Don't worry if a sheet tears as you can easily patch up any damage – only the top 2 sheets need to stay undamaged.

Place a sheet of filo/phyllo in the baking pan. (Cover the remaining sheets with clingfilm/plastic wrap to prevent them from drying out.) Brush oil lightly over the sheet. Cover with another sheet and oil it. Repeat this process with 2 more sheets.

Spread one-fifth of the filling evenly over the top with a spatula. Cover with one sheet, oil lightly and cover with a second sheet (this one doesn't need oiling). Spread one-fifth of the filling evenly over the top. Continue like this until you have used up all the filling, and you have 5 layers each of filling and filo/phyllo sheets.

To finish, brush a little oil over the remaining 5 sheets of filo/phyllo and lay them on top of the pie – the 2 best, undamaged sheets should be on the top. Tuck in any pastry or filling sticking out of the pan by pushing a spatula between the pie and the sides of the pan. Use a sharp knife to score 12 squares into the pastry.

Bake in the preheated oven for 45 minutes, or until the top turns golden brown and the pie isn't wobbly or soft to the touch. Allow to cool completely (at least 5 hours, or overnight) in the pan before serving.

CHAPTER 7

Special baked treats

For desserts, festive feasts and family recipes to hand down through the generations – special baked treats will delight anyone who's lucky enough to try them. These treasured celebratory recipes will stay long in the memory of any guest, vegan or not, and inspire them to bake vegan in their own home.

My mum used to make sweet, baked pancakes a lot when I was a kid and it is still one of my favourite dishes. Today when I make it, I replace the eggs and fresh cheese with tofu and non-dairy cream and it tastes the same, if not better! It's a light dessert but we even eat it instead of lunch – a feast for every kid who prefers sweet food to savoury!

Baked, lemon-scented pancakes

FOR THE PANCAKES

340 ml/1½ cups plain soy milk

¼ teaspoon salt

¼ teaspoon baking powder

grated zest of 1 lemon

215 g/1⅔ cups unbleached plain/all-purpose flour

coconut or sunflower oil, for frying

FOR THE FILLING

340 g/2 cups plain, firm tofu

685 ml/3 cups thick soy or oat cream

a pinch of salt

freshly squeezed juice of 2 lemons

grated zest of 3 lemons, plus extra to garnish

brown rice or agave syrup, to taste

30–60 g/¼–½ cup raisins (optional)

23 x 30 cm/9 x 12-in. baking pan or ovenproof dish, oiled

Serves 4–6

For the pancakes, mix the milk and 225 ml/1 cup water in a bowl. Stir in the salt, baking powder and lemon zest. Gradually add the flour, whisking vigorously until smooth. The batter should be thicker than conventional, egg-based pancake batter. Allow to rest for at least 15 minutes.

Heat a heavy-based frying pan and brush a little oil over it. When hot, pour a small ladle of batter into the pan and tilt the pan to spread the batter evenly over the surface. Once the edges start turning golden brown, flip the pancake over and cook until golden on the reverse. Transfer to a plate, re-oil the pan and keep making pancakes in this way until all the batter is used up. Try to make the pancakes quite thin and that should give you 10 pancakes in total.

Preheat the oven to 180°C (350°F) Gas 4.

For the filling, put the tofu, 225 ml/1 cup of the cream, the salt, lemon juice and zest and syrup, to taste, in a food processor and blend until smooth. Mix in the raisins: they give a lovely tangy flavour to this dish, but you can omit them and add a little more syrup, if you wish.

Divide the filling between the pancakes, spreading it over each one. Roll the pancakes up tightly and arrange in the prepared baking pan. Pour the remaining cream evenly over the pancakes and garnish with some lemon zest.

Bake in the preheated oven for 15–20 minutes, until golden. Serve warm or cold as preferred.

What could be more tempting than soft dough filled with tasty fruit, nuts or chocolate? They are great for breakfast or between meals and they're very practical for kids' (or adults') lunchboxes. I like to keep things simple, so I mostly use homemade jam as a filling, but for special occasions I use a nut-based or melted chocolate filling and shape the dough into pockets, rolls or roses!

Pockets and roses with sweet fillings

FOR THE DOUGH

300 g/2⅓ cups strong unbleached bread flour

30 g/¼ cup strong wholemeal/whole-wheat flour

5 g/1 teaspoon active dry yeast (additive-free)

¼ teaspoon salt

a pinch of ground turmeric

150 ml/⅔ cup plain soy milk

40 g/2 tablespoons non-hydrogenated margarine

1 tablespoon sunflower oil

2 tablespoons brown rice syrup, plus extra for brushing

FOR THE FILLING

180 g/1 full cup toasted hazelnuts, finely ground, or 320 g/1¼ cups naturally sweetened fruit jam

130 g/½ cup brown rice syrup

1 tablespoon carob powder

1-2 tablespoons non-dairy milk, if needed

baking sheet, lined with parchment paper

Makes about 16

For the dough, mix together the flours, yeast, salt and turmeric. Heat the milk in a saucepan until hot, then add the margarine and stir until melted. Add the oil and syrup. Pour into the bowl of dry ingredients and mix with a wooden spoon to get a smooth lump of dough. Transfer to a floured surface and knead vigorously for at least 3 minutes. Place in an oiled bowl, cover with a wet towel and allow to rise for 90 minutes. Punch it down and allow to rise for another 30 minutes.

Preheat the oven to 180°C (350°F) Gas 4.

For the filling, mix the ingredients to get a spreadable paste.

To make 'pockets', roll out the dough on a lightly floured surface until about 2–3 mm/⅛ inch thick and allow to rest like that for 5 minutes. Stamp out as many rounds as you can with a thin glass or cookie cutter about 8.5 cm/3¼ inches in diameter. Re-roll any trimmings and stamp out more rounds. Place 1 scant tablespoon filling in the middle of each circle. Dip your finger in water and run it around the edge of the pastry round. Fold in half, enclosing the filling, and press the edges together firmly all the way around. Arrange on the prepared baking sheet.

To make 'roses', divide the dough in 3 equal portions. Roll each into a long strip about 2–3 mm/⅛ inch thick, then spread the filling thinly along one long edge. Roll the dough up carefully around the filling and into a sausage. Cut each roll into about 12 slices. Lay on the prepared baking sheet, cut side up.

Bake the 'pockets' or 'roses' in the preheated oven for 15 minutes or until golden. Brush syrup over them while still warm.

These are best eaten the same day but they are still delicious the next 1–2 days. Store in an airtight container.

There is a myth going around that Easter buns are very tricky to make and that you must be an experienced baker to get it right without adding a couple of eggs to the dough. That's why I delayed trying them for a long time, thinking it must be the most difficult thing in the world, but it wasn't. I took my nonna's recipe, and after a couple of half-successful tries I got it right. So here's a vegan Easter bun recipe that you can (and should) make throughout the year, not only for Easter!

Sugar-free Italian Easter buns

sunflower oil, for brushing

FOR THE STARTER
6 tablespoons plain soy milk, lukewarm
9 g/2 teaspoons active dry yeast (additive-free)
25 g/2 tablespoons rice, pure maple or agave syrup
2 tablespoons strong unbleached bread flour

FOR THE DOUGH
40 g/⅓ cup unsulfured dried apricots, chopped
40 g/⅓ cup raisins
3 tablespoons rum
grated zest of 1 orange
500 g/4 cups strong unbleached bread flour or unbleached spelt flour
½ teaspoon salt
⅛ teaspoon ground turmeric
170 ml/¾ cup plain soy milk
100 g/¾ cup non-hydrogenated margarine
2 teaspoons vanilla extract
65 g/¼ cup rice, pure maple or agave syrup, plus extra for brushing
baking sheet, lined with parchment paper

Makes 3 large buns

Mix together the starter ingredients in a mixing bowl, cover and allow to rest for 30 minutes or until doubled in size.

For the dough, mix together the apricots, raisins, rum and orange zest in a bowl and allow to soak while the starter is rising.

Sift together the flour, salt and tumeric in a bowl.

Heat the milk in a saucepan until hot, then add the margarine and stir until melted. Add the vanilla extract and syrup, then the soaked fruit as well as the starter. Mix well. Pour into the flour mix and combine with a wooden spoon to get a smooth lump of dough. Transfer to a floured surface and knead vigorously for at least 5 minutes, until silky and elastic. Place in an oiled bowl, cover with a wet kitchen towel and allow to rise in a warm spot for 2½ hours or until doubled in size.

Punch down the dough, give it a quick knead, then divide it into three equal portions. Shape each into a ball and put on the prepared baking sheet. Snip V-shaped cuts into the top of each loaf so that they open up during baking. Cover well with a kitchen towel and allow to rise again for 30 minutes or until doubled in size.

Preheat the oven to 200°C (400°F) Gas 6.

Brush a little oil over the buns and bake in the preheated oven for 30–60 minutes or until golden. Brush syrup over them while still hot, then transfer to a wire rack to cool.

These should be stored wrapped in a kitchen towel in a cool and dry place and will keep for a week or a little longer.

These aren't exactly my nonna's crescent rolls, but her old recipe inspired me to make a vegan version since they were a big part of our Christmases. There used to be a giant bowl full of them, carefully rolled in icing/confectioners' sugar, hidden away in one of the cold bedrooms where we (me and my cousins) weren't really allowed to go. But we would steal a couple whenever we could, and hoped nonna wouldn't notice!

My nonna's crescent rolls

FOR THE STARTER
110 ml/½ cup lukewarm plain soy milk
20 g/½ cube fresh (compressed) yeast
2 tablespoons brown rice syrup

FOR THE DOUGH
400 g/3 cups strong unbleached bread flour
¼ teaspoon bourbon vanilla powder
¼ teaspoon salt
250 g/1⅔ cups non-hydrogenated margarine, at room temperature
2 tablespoons brown rice syrup

FOR THE FILLING
120 ml/½ cup non-dairy milk
25 g/2 rows of vegan dark/bittersweet chocolate, finely chopped
250 g/2¾ cups finely ground walnuts
5 tablespoons brown rice syrup, plus extra for brushing

baking sheets, lined with parchment paper

Makes about 48

For the starter, whisk the milk, yeast and syrup together in a small bowl, cover and allow to rest for 30 minutes. The yeast will start to foam slightly while it is resting.

For the dough, in a separate bowl, mix together the flour, vanilla and salt, add the margarine and mix in with your fingertips to get a crumbly texture. Add the syrup, mix well, then add the bubbly yeast mixture. Transfer to a lightly floured surface and knead until smooth – about 5 minutes. Shape into a ball and allow to rest at room temperature while you make the filling.

For the filling, heat the milk in a saucepan over medium heat, then add the chocolate and stir until melted. Add the walnuts and syrup and whisk over low heat for 1–2 minutes.

Divide the dough into 4 equal portions. Put one portion of dough on a sheet of parchment paper. Roll out with a rolling pin into a rough circle about 2 mm/¹⁄₃₂ inch thick. Use a pastry wheel to cut the circle into 12 equal wedges – the circle should now look like a bicycle wheel.

Divide the filling into 48 equal portions – about 1 big teaspoon each. Place a portion of filling horizontally along the base of each dough triangle, then roll up loosely towards the pointed end. Place each roll, point side down, onto a prepared baking sheet. Allow to rest at room temperature for 15 minutes.

Preheat the oven to 180°C (350°F) Gas 4.

Bake the rolls in the preheated oven for 15–20 minutes or until lightly golden. Brush syrup over them while still hot, then transfer to a wire rack to cool. Or roll them in icing/confectioners' sugar if you really, really want to.

Store in an airtight container for a week or a little longer.

The best plums to use here are Italian plums or any small variety that can easily be pitted. You can also use small apricots, frozen plums or even fruit jam as a filling. It's a time-consuming recipe but I never regret a minute spent making it!

Plum dumplings

800 g/4 medium russet potatoes, scrubbed clean

2 tablespoons non-hydrogenated margarine

75 ml/⅓ cup plain soy milk

40 ml/3 tablespoons soy or oat cream

2¾ teaspoons salt

200 g/1½ cups unbleached plain/all-purpose flour, plus plenty extra for kneading

5 tablespoons sunflower oil

95 g/1 cup fine breadcrumbs

¼ teaspoon ground cinnamon

480 g/16 small plums, eg. Italian prune plums

110 g/16 teaspoons pure maple syrup, plus extra for serving

Makes 16

Boil the potatoes in their skins until very tender. Drain, allow to cool a little, then peel. (This is the best way to boil potatoes for dumplings, but if you don't have time, peel them, cut into chunks and boil until very tender.) Mash them well until free of lumps but do not blend them in a food processor otherwise they will turn gluey!

Put the margarine, milk and cream in a small saucepan and heat over low heat until the margarine has melted. Add ¾ teaspoon salt and whisk well. Stir gradually into the mashed potatoes to make a thick mash. Stir in the flour and mix thoroughly.

Turn the dough out onto a floured surface and knead in a little extra flour (up to 130 g/1 cup) until the dough is quite soft but doesn't stick to your hands. It should weigh about 1.15 kg/2½ lb. Divide it in 4 equal portions and roll each one into a fat sausage. Place on a floured tray and refrigerate for 30 minutes.

Meanwhile, heat the oil in a frying pan, add the breadcrumbs and stir continuously over medium heat until golden brown. Transfer to a large plate and mix in the cinnamon.

Carefully start to slice each plum in half around the pit but don't halve it completely – you just want to remove the pit and leave the plum whole.

Bring a large saucepan of water to a slow boil and add the remaining salt. Preheat the oven to 180°C (350°F) Gas 4.

Take the dough out of the fridge. With your palms, flatten each sausage into a 24 x 8-cm/9½ x 3½-inch strip. Cut each strip into 4 squares. Fill each plum with one teaspoon maple syrup and place on a square, trying not to let the syrup escape. Bring the corners up and around the plum. Pinch the seams together tightly to seal.

Gently drop about 4 dumplings into the pan of boiling water. Once they float to the surface, cook for about 5 minutes. Take out, drain well and roll each dumpling in the breadcrumbs until coated. Cook all the remaining dumplings in this way. Serve warm with syrup drizzled over them.

Index

agar 15
agave syrup 13
almonds: couscous and jam crunchies 78
aluminium-free baking powder 15
apples: apple, poppy-seed and walnut pie 107
breakfast muffins with apples and jam 24
European-style apple pie 92
summer muffins with raspberries and blackberries 28
apricots: apricot and chocolate bites 74
apricot and tofu cheesecake 95
sugar-free Italian Easter buns 136
aromatic pear strudel 104

baking powder, aluminium-free 15
baking soda 15
baklava rolls 108
bananas: marbled energy muffins 27
barley malt 11
bars see slices and bars
bean and cashew brownies 66
bicarbonate of/baking soda 15
biscotti, pistachio and fennel 86
biscuits see cookies and biscuits
black and white cake with lemon buttercream 49
black-forest-gâteau cupcakes 50
blackberries, summer muffins with raspberries and 28
bread: focaccia dough 20
grissini with caraway seeds 120
herb focaccia 115
no-knead everyday bread 112
25-minute cornbread 119
breakfast muffins with apples and jam 24
brown rice syrup 11

brownies, bean and cashew 66
buns: pockets and roses with sweet fillings 135
sugar-free Italian Easter buns 136
buttercream frosting: cocoa 46
lemon 49

cakes: basic chocolate cake 18
basic nut cake 19
castagnaccio 32
hazelnut heaven cake 45
pan di spagna 31
sweet-potato pound cake 35
troubleshooting 16
see also fancy cakes
caraway seeds, grissini with 120
carob slices 58
carrot cake, rich 54
cashews: bean and cashew brownies 66
rich tea bread 36
spicy oat cookies with cashews 77
castagnaccio 32
chard: soparnik pies with onions and greens 123
cheesecake, apricot and tofu 95
cherries: black-forest-gâteau cupcakes 50
fruit-topped bars 65
chestnut flour 8
castagnaccio 32
chocolate: apricot and chocolate bites 74
basic chocolate cake 18
bean and cashew brownies 66
black-forest-gâteau cupcakes 50
chocolate cream 42
chocolate ganache tart 103
chocolate layer cake 42
cocoa buttercream frosting 46
double cocoa and strawberry cake 46
marbled energy muffins 27
my Nonna's crescent rolls 139
pockets and roses with sweet fillings 135
sticky mocha squares 61

see also carob
cocoa see chocolate
coconut: apricot and chocolate bites 74
exotic pineapple and coconut cake 53
lamingtons 69
my favourite coconut cookies 81
raffaello slices 62
rich carrot cake 54
coconut milk 15
coconut oil 14
coffee: coffee toffee cookies 89
sticky mocha squares 61
cookies and biscuits 73–89
apricot and chocolate bites 74
coffee toffee cookies 89
couscous and jam crunchies 78
Dad's hazelnut triangles 85
drop cookies with persimmon and cranberries 82
my favourite coconut cookies 81
pistachio and fennel biscotti 86
spicy oat cookies with cashews 77
troubleshooting 16–17
corn and tofu pie 128
cornflour (cornmeal) 8
25-minute cornbread 119
quinoa scones 39
couscous 8
couscous and jam crunchies 78
crackers: cracker snacks with black sesame seeds 124
rye and olive-oil crackers 116
cranberries: drop cookies with persimmon and cranberries 82
rich tea bread 36
cream: chocolate cream 42
hazelnut cream 45
troubleshooting 17
crescent rolls, my Nonna's 139
crumble, peach 96
cupcakes, black-forest-gâteau 50

Dad's hazelnut triangles 85
dates: rich tea bread 36

double cocoa and strawberry cake 46
dried fruit: quinoa scones 39
see also apricots; figs; raisins
drop cookies with persimmon and cranberries 82
dumplings, plum 140

Easter buns, Italian 136
energy muffins, marbled 27
European-style apple pie 92
exotic pineapple and coconut cake 53
extra virgin olive oil 13

fancy cakes 41–55
black and white cake with lemon buttercream 49
black-forest-gâteau cupcakes 50
chocolate layer cake 42
double cocoa and strawberry cake 46
exotic pineapple and coconut cake 53
hazelnut heaven cake 45
rich carrot cake 54
farina see semolina
fennel seeds: pistachio and fennel biscotti 86
figs: pan di spagna 31
filo/phyllo pastry 8
flours 8
focaccia dough 20
herb focaccia 115
frostings: cocoa buttercream 46
lemon buttercream 49
troubleshooting 17
see also glazes
fruit: fresh fruit tartlets 100
fruit-topped bars 65
see also apples, strawberries etc

glazes: carob glaze 58
see also frosting
grissini with caraway seeds 120

hazelnuts: castagnaccio 32
Dad's hazelnut triangles 85
fruit-topped bars 65
hazelnut heaven cake 45
peach crumble 96

pockets and roses with
sweet fillings 135
rich tea bread 36
healthier baklava rolls
108
herb focaccia 115

ingredients 8–15
Italian Easter buns 136

jam: breakfast muffins with
apples and jam 24
couscous and jam
crunchies 78
oat bars filled with jam 70
pockets and roses with
sweet fillings 135

kumquats: black and white
cake with lemon
buttercream 49

lamingtons 69
lemon: baked, lemon-
scented pancakes 132
black and white cake with
lemon buttercream 49

malt, barley 11
maple syrup 13
plum dumplings 140
marbled energy muffins
27
margarine, non-
hydrogenated 14
milks, non-dairy 14–15
mocha squares, sticky 61
muffins: breakfast muffins
with apples and jam 24
marbled energy muffins
27
summer muffins with
raspberries and
blackberries 28
my favourite coconut
cookies 81
my Nonna's crescent rolls
139

navy beans: bean and
cashew brownies 66
no-knead everyday bread
112
nuts: basic nut cake 19
nut milks 15
see also hazelnuts,
walnuts etc

oat milk 15
oats: no-knead everyday
bread 112

oat bars filled with jam 70
peach crumble 96
spicy oat cookies with
cashews 77
oils 13–14
olive oil 13
rye and olive-oil crackers
116
onions, soparnik pies with
greens and 123
oranges: rich carrot cake 54

pan di spagna 31
pancakes: baked, lemon-
scented 132
pastry snails with spicy
pumpkin filling 127
peach crumble 96
pear strudel 104
persimmon, drop cookies
with cranberries and 82
phyllo pastry 8
aromatic pear strudel 104
corn and tofu pie 128
healthier baklava rolls 108
troubleshooting 17
pie crust: sweet pie dough
20
troubleshooting 16
pies: apple, poppy-seed
and walnut pie 107
corn and tofu pie 128
European-style apple pie
92
pastry snails with spicy
pumpkin filling 127
soparnik pies with onions
and greens 123
pine nuts: castagnaccio 32
pan di spagna 31
pineapple: exotic
pineapple and coconut
cake 53
pistachio and fennel
biscotti 86
pizza dough 20
plant-based milks 15
plums: plum dumplings 140
plum crostata 99
rich tea bread 36
pockets and roses with
sweet fillings 135
polenta: quinoa scones 39
poppy seeds: apple,
poppy-seed and walnut
pie 107
potatoes: plum dumplings
140
pound cake, sweet-potato
35
problems 16–17

pumpkin: pastry snails with
spicy pumpkin filling 127

quinoa scones 39

raffaello slices 62
raising agents 15
raisins: baked, lemon-
scented pancakes 132
breakfast muffins with
apples and jam 24
castagnaccio 32
European-style apple pie
92
rich carrot cake 54
rich tea bread 36
sugar-free Italian Easter
buns 136
raspberries, summer
muffins with blackberries
and 28
rice milk 15
rice syrup 11
rich carrot cake 54
rich tea bread 36
rolls, my Nonna's crescent
139
roses with sweet fillings 135
rye and olive-oil crackers
116

safflower oil 13–14
scones, quinoa 39
seed milks 15
semolina (farina) 8
sesame seeds, cracker
snacks with 124
slices and bars 57–71
bean and cashew
brownies 66
fruit-topped bars 65
lamingtons 69
oat bars filled with jam 70
raffaello slices 62
sticky mocha squares 61
yummy carob slices 58
soparnik pies with onions
and greens 123
soy milk 14–15
spelt flour 8
spicy oat cookies with
cashews 77
sticky mocha squares 61
strawberries: double cocoa
and strawberry cake 46
strudel, aromatic pear 104
sugar 10–11
addiction to 10
unrefined sugars 13
sugar-free Italian Easter
buns 136

summer muffins with
raspberries and
blackberries 28
sunflower oil 13
sweet corn: corn and tofu
pie 128
sweet pie dough 20
sweet-potato pound cake
35
sweeteners 10–13

tarts: chocolate ganache
tart 103
fresh fruit tartlets 100
plum crostata 99
troubleshooting 16
tea bread, rich 36
thickeners 15
toffee: coffee toffee
cookies 89
tofu: apple, poppy-seed
and walnut pie 107
apricot and tofu
cheesecake 95
baked, lemon-scented
pancakes 132
chocolate ganache tart
103
corn and tofu pie 128
sweet-potato pound cake
35
troubleshooting 16–17
25-minute cornbread 119

unbleached wheat flour 8
unrefined sugars 13

vanilla-pineapple cream 53
virgin coconut oil 14
virgin olive oil 13

walnuts: apple, poppy-seed
and walnut pie 107
drop cookies with
persimmon and
cranberries 82
healthier baklava rolls 108
my Nonna's crescent rolls
139
pan di spagna 31
rich carrot cake 54
rich tea bread 36
wheat flour 8
wholemeal/whole-wheat
flour 8

yeast 51
troubleshooting 17
yummy carob slices 58

Acknowledgements

I'd like to thank:

Lisa Clayton, THE fairy – thanks for being at the right place at the right time and for spreading the word about my cooking adventures!

Ivor Somrak, THE husband – thank you so, so much for your loving words of support, loving hugs, and loving foot massages I needed badly after all the testing I did for this cookbook! Also, for designing me the coolest website ever! www.rentajchefa.com

Nada and Branko, THE parents – growing up surrounded by your art and creativity made me realize how important it is to do what you love, no matter how hard it can sometimes be. Thank you!

Irena and Boris Somrak, THE in-laws – without your love and support I wouldn't have been able to achieve so much in the past couple of years. Thank you for being there for me.

Fumica and Milena, THE grandmas – you both made me fall in love with cooking and baking and I cannot thank you enough for that.

Jadranka and Zlatko Peji – for offering me my first vegan baking job. That opportunity made me realize how much I really loved baking.

Everybody at Ryland Peters & Small – you made this book as beautiful as it is, and Céline Hughes, you are definitely THE commissioning editor!

Ivana and Melani, THE girlfriends – thank you for being there for me for most of my life!

All my other beautiful friends, students, clients and Facebook fans – your support of my work and the daily feedback I get keep me motivated to work even harder! Thank you all!

And last but not least, my dear cat Bu, THE pet – you kept me company during long baking nights and never failed to show interest in what was going on in the oven. Your burnt whiskers are proof of your support of my work!